HEINEMANN
NEW WINDMILLS

THE RUNAWAYS

It is a stormy February day. The sky is laden with storm clouds, and the rain is sheeting down. Young Samuel Miles – better known as Smiler – has a problem. He is under police escort, on his way to the station. His father is the only person who can help him, and he is away at sea.

Smiler's only chance is to run away and hide until his father is back to sort out the mess. So when lightning strikes and gives Smiler a chance to get away, he makes his dash for freedom.

Ten miles down the road, at Longleat, Yarra the cheetah is strangely restless. She stalks the boundary fence, unable to settle. Suddenly a great bolt of lightning flattens the fence. Like Smiler, Yarra has found her freedom . . .

VICTOR CANNING

The Runaways

HEINEMANN
NEW WINDMILLS

Heinemann Educational Books Ltd
Halley Court, Jordan Hill, Oxford OX2 8EJ
OXFORD   LONDON   EDINBURGH
MELBOURNE   SYDNEY   AUCKLAND
IBADAN   NAIROBI   GABORONE   HARARE
KINGSTON   PORTSMOUTH NH (USA)
SINGAPORE   MADRID

ISBN 0 435 12180 4

90 91 92 93 94 95 18 17 16 15 14 13 12 11 10 9

Printed in England by Clays Ltd, St Ives plc

For Duncan, now;
and Hugo, later.

Contents

1	LIGHTNING STRIKES TWICE	1
2	SHELTER FOR TWO	12
3	A DOOR IS CLOSED	26
4	A DOOR IS OPENED	40
5	A CHANGE OF COLOUR AND NAME	57
6	YARRA MOVES ON	83
7	THE LOST VILLAGE	102
8	A HAPPY EVENT—AND OTHERS	119
9	A CHANGE OF LODGINGS	133
10	ENQUIRIES ARE BEING MADE	151
11	TWO MOTHERS MEET	167
12	SMILER TAKES CHARGE	182
13	THE SLEEP-WALKER	196
14	HAIL AND FAREWELL	214

I

ᨆ *Lightning Strikes Twice* ᨆ

It had been raining all night, and all the morning; raining hard all over Dorset, Wiltshire and Hampshire. It was a cold February rain, filling the ditches, swelling the rivers, and stripping the few dead leaves that still clung to the trees. It made quagmires of the cow treads at field gates, spouted over blocked gutters, and flooded the low-lying roads so that passing cars sent up bow waves of spray and soaked unlucky passers-by. Now, at half-past eleven precisely, as Smiler was being driven in a police car under the escort of two burly patrol men, the father and mother of a thunder and lightning storm was brewing overhead. At first it was a few little murmurs, slowly rising to a full-scale roll and rumble of heavy thunder. Suddenly there came a great stabbing, downward sword thrust of lightning that turned the whole world into a blue and yellow dazzle of light.

Smiler jumped in his seat and cried, "Blimey!"

The policeman alongside him smiled. He said, "Nothing to be scared of, son. Just think – if we hadn't picked you up, you'd be out in it soaked even more." He glanced at Smiler's pile of wet clothes on the floor of the car and then at the blanket-wrapped figure.

It was a red, yellow and green striped blanket and all that could be seen of Smiler was his head sticking out of the top, his fair hair still wet. Smiler – real name Samuel Miles – was fifteen years and five months old. He had escaped two weeks before from an approved school, and had been picked up that morning by the police. He had been caught because of a tip from a farmer in whose barn he had been hiding (and whose hens' eggs he had been eating, sucking them raw).

Smiler wasn't scared. The lightning had just made him jump, that was all. It took quite a lot to make Smiler scared. Smiler could look after himself. He was tallish and well-built with a friendly, squarish face, a pressed-in smudge of a nose, and a pair of angelic blue eyes that, when he put on his special smile, made him look as though butter wouldn't melt in his mouth. But if Smiler didn't scare easily there were also a lot of things Smiler didn't like.

Smiler didn't like school, for instance. Particularly he didn't like approved school and he had run away from it after exactly thirteen days' and four hours' residence. Smiler didn't much care for the country either – not because it scared him or he felt out of place there (Smiler could always make himself at home in new surroundings). He just preferred towns and cities where there were more opportunities for picking up the odds and ends of things that made living tolerable.

After all, when you were mostly on your own, you had to eat and drink, have a bit of money in your pocket and be able to go to the cinema now and then and treat yourself to a Coke in a café when you felt like company.

Most of all, he didn't like the long periods when his father went off to sea. Then, instead of living in lodgings with his father and having a wonderful time, he was always dumped with Sister Ethel and her husband, Albert. Smiler didn't like living with his married sister and her husband. Not because he didn't like them. They were all right except when they were fussy about their house and their furniture and grumbled because his hands always marked the paintwork. Also, Smiler didn't like being idle. He liked doing things. He liked to be busy. The trouble was that people made such a fuss about some of the things he did. . . . Well, like pinching a bottle of milk from a doorstep if he was thirsty, or nicking a comic book from a shop if he felt like reading.

The driver, eyeing Smiler's reflection in the interior mirror, grinned and said, "You look like a red Indian in that blanket. Little Chief Sitting Bull."

At that moment, two hundred yards ahead of the car, a streak of lightning flared earthwards. It seared itself into the top branches of a tree at the roadside, wreathed its way down the trunk and hit the ground with a crack that made the whole earth shake. A great branch was split from the top of the tree and crashed across the road, blocking it. The police car braked and skidded to a halt twenty yards from the obstruction. A small car coming in the opposite direction was not so lucky. The branch fell a few yards in front of the car. The driver braked hard and the car slewed sideways into the block.

The two policemen, alert as all good policemen should be in an emergency, jumped out of the patrol car and dashed through the rain to give assistance to the driver of the other car who, as a matter of fact, was more shaken and shocked than injured. It took the two policemen a good three or four minutes to climb over the obstruction and to assure themselves that the driver was in no great distress. It took the driver of the patrol car another few minutes to get back to the car so that he could send out a call to headquarters reporting the road blockage and summoning assistance.

As he sent out the radio call, he knew that the moment he had finished he would have to add another – reporting the escape again from custody of one Samuel Miles. In the car mirror as he sent his report the policeman could see the back seat. The only evidence that Smiler had ever sat there was a damp patch on the leather. Smiler had gone, his pile of clothes had gone, and so had the blanket!

Smiler at that moment was three hundred yards away running barefooted along the side of a ploughed field, pelting up the slight slope to a crest of woodland which he could just glimpse through the driving sheets of rain. He ran holding his hands round the tucked up edges of the blanket, his naked legs and thighs mud and rain splattered. All his clothes and his shoes were gathered in front of him in the blanket.

As Smiler kept running he was smiling to himself because he was free. This time – because there were some lessons he only had to be given once to remember – he meant to stay free. Just what he would do with his freedom he didn't know – except that he was going to enjoy it until his father got back from sea. When his father returned he knew he would quickly clear up the whole mess and mis-understanding that had sent him off to reform school. And heaven alone knew where his father

4

was at this moment, somewhere on the high seas, cooking away for the crew or maybe giving them a tune from his mouth-organ on the after-deck.

As Smiler disappeared into the rain-shrouded countryside, the second policeman returned to the car, took one look at the back seat and said, "He's hopped it!"

"Gone," said the other. "With our blanket. Do we go after him?"

"In this weather? And with this mess on the road? Not likely. Anyway, he won't get far when the call goes out for him." The policeman grinned and said jokingly, "Wanted, Little Chief Sitting Bull. Height five feet two inches, fair-haired, blue-eyed, age fifteen plus, wearing a red, green and yellow blanket – or wet blue jeans, grey shirt and brown jacket. Approach with caution. This man is dangerous." He paused, thought for a moment, and added, "I forgot. Addition to description. Wanted person's face is heavily freckled."

"Funny thing," said the other, "you don't often see boys with such freckled faces these days, do you? They seem to have gone out of fashion or something."

As the two policemen went back to the road block to try and clear it, Smiler reached the cover of the woods at the top of the hill. He crashed into the undergrowth like a rocket and put up a couple of pheasants that flew away, honking and screeching with alarm. The noise so startled Smiler that he slipped and fell flat on his face. Because of the effort of his clumsy running and the loss of the little wind he had left from the fall, he lay there panting like a stranded fish. For the few moments while he rested, getting his breath back, Smiler gave himself a

5

talking-to. He was a great one for talking to himself in moments of crisis. He lectured himself now, face close to the wet, leaf-littered ground.

"Samuel M.," he said (Smiler was other people's name for him and he didn't care much for it. It was a silly kind of punning joke on his name. He preferred Samuel M. because that was what his father called him.), "you got to think this out. You're wet and muddy and half naked. Your clothes is all soaked and your belly's rumbling a bit now and then because all you've had in the last two days is them eggs just raw and nothing to write home about. You are wanted by the police. Like a real criminal, which you aren't. It was never you that took the old lady's handbag. Thing Number One, then. Them cops down there won't follow you, not in this weather with that accident to look after. Good. Thing Number Two. You got to get warmed up, fed, and into hiding. You got to look for a safe and sheltered anchorage where you can get everything stowed shipshape and work out a new course. And, Thing Number Three is, you'd better get them wet clothes on. Just wearing a coloured blanket is going to make you stand out like a catherine wheel against a tarred fence."

So Smiler got to his feet. Stark naked under the leaden, rain-deluging sky, he began to pull on his wet blue jeans. As he struggled with them, hissing with effort through his teeth at their awkwardness, there was a massive bellow of thunder from away to the west and the whole sky was lit with another blaze of lightning, slashing earthwards. This time, though Smiler could not know it, the lightning was doing exactly the same for another prisoner

6

as the previous bolt from the blue had done for him.

*   *   *

Ten miles away, northwest of the wood in which Smiler was dressing and about four miles a little southwest of the Wiltshire town of Warminster, was the large country estate and ancestral home of the Marquis of Bath. The mansion was called Longleat House and the estates around it Longleat Park. Part of the park had been turned into a wild animal reserve. Every day of the year cars rolled into Longleat Park bringing tourists to see the treasures of the beautiful Longleat House and also to see the Lions of Longleat and the other animals which were kept in huge, penned-in stretches of the parkland. Every day cars moved around the road which twisted and twined through the high-fenced animal enclosures.

The road ran first through the East African section which held giraffes, zebras, ostriches, and antelopes; and then on through the monkey jungle with its baboons that often cadged free rides on top of the cars; and so into the lion reserve where the kings of beasts sometimes lay lazily across the roadway refusing to move out of the path of the cars until the mood took them. Finally the car procession entered the cheetah area.

Today because it was February, and a storm- and rain-filled day, there were no more than three or four cars in the whole animal reserve. At this moment there was none in the cheetah section. In fact, there were few animals out in the enclosures either. They no more liked the rain and the storm than human beings. The baboons were in their dugouts and the lions in their wooden pens or stretched out on the sheltered verandahs of their huts. In the cheetah reserve all the cheetahs were under shelter in their huts – all, except one.

This cheetah was a female. Her name was Yarra. All the cheetahs in the enclosures had names. . . Apollo, Chester, Lotus, Suki, Tina and Schultz. Yarra was a full grown female. She weighed a hundred and thirty pounds. She stood nearly three feet high to her narrow, raking shoulders and from the point of her black nose to the tip of her long tufted tail she measured seven feet and one inch. Yarra was a good-tempered animal. She had been captured as a cub in Africa, brought to Germany and from there to Longleat Park.

She was a magnificent animal. Under the rain the spots on her tawny orange coat were as black as small wet coals. The dark lines of her face maskings, running from inside the eyes down around her muzzle, were boldly drawn charcoal lines. Her throat and underbelly were creamy white, and her eyes tawny gold. As she moved she swung her long tail from side to side, flicking little sprays of rain from the tuft at its end.

When the Cheetah Warden came into the enclosure in his Land-Rover and Yarra felt in the mood she could jump in one easy long-flowing movement to the top of the driving cab. Sometimes, to give the cheetahs exercise, the warden towed a trail rope from the back of the Land-Rover with a piece of meat tied to it for the cheetahs to chase. Even though he accelerated to forty miles an hour Yarra could easily keep up. If he had gone at sixty miles an hour she could have held pace with the car for a while.

Today Yarra was strangely restless. The rain and the thunder and lightning had increased her restlessness. It was not the restlessness that overcame her and the other cheetahs when, from time to time, they marked with their keen sight the movement of guinea fowl, partridge, pheasant or young deer moving on the free slopes of the parkland outside the enclosure. At those times they raced to the wire fence, longing for the freedom of the hunt and the chase, only to turn back and stalk the length of the wire, stubby ears alert, the desire for complete liberty moving hot and strong through their powerful bodies.

Now, something else had made Yarra restless and she did not know what it was. All she knew was that where normally she would have taken shelter from the rain, she now wanted to remain outside, moving up and down the long line of the boundary fence. Up and down, up and down she stalked. The fence was strong and made of two-inch iron mesh. It was over twelve feet high with an inwards overhang at the top, and it was supported on strong wooden poles with here and there a large concrete support to give added strength. Inside the outer fence, a few feet from it, was another fence, about four feet high. Yarra and any of the other cheetahs could have jumped this inner fence easily, but they never did. What was the point of jumping this fence when it was clear that the outer one was a barrier that could never be overleaped?

There was a low rumble of thunder from above and a stronger burst of rain that slashed into Yarra's face. She sat down on her haunches close to the inner fence, shook her head and blinked her eyes against the rain scud. She remained there, sitting upright like a sphinx, her eyes on the long grass slope outside the high fence, marking the low flight across it of a bedraggled rook. The slope ran upwards to a patch of ploughed land and then on to a wood that marked its crest. Here and there a fir tree stood out stark, glossy green against the February blackness of the other trees.

Another rumble of thunder broke out above and Yarra moved on, her restlessness eating into her. She lowered her fore quarters almost to the ground. Raking with her hind legs at the wet and muddy grass, she sent little clods of earth flying into the air. She turned her head sideways, seeing the cheetah hut at the bottom of the enclosure. Closer was a great fallen oak tree which the cheetahs used as their playground. She opened her jaws, flexing the skin back over her teeth and gums, and gave a long half-snarling, half-hissing sound that ended in a short, snapping spit.

It was at this moment, as Smiler was pulling up his wet jeans over a wet shirt ten miles away, that the sky above burst with an earth-shaking roar of thunder. A great bolt of lightning was loosed through the low-hanging clouds, setting the grey day ablaze with vivid light.

The lightning hit the outer fence of the cheetah enclosure ten yards below Yarra. It ran in an exploding aura of blue fire the length of the wire mesh. It found the metal bolts in a concrete support and ripped fence and support from the ground as though a great hand had smashed and flung them down. The falling top half of the support flattened the low inner fence a yard from Yarra. She leapt, snarling with fright, into the air. Her nostrils were charged with the smell of burning from the lightning strike. She came down from her panic bound on top of the collapsed outer section of the boundary fence. As thunder rolled angrily again she was gone, her whole body, every nerve in her, impelled by fear and shock. She streaked away up the grassy slope towards the wood in a wild, fast-leaping run, moving like a tawny-gold streak at top speed.

Within thirty seconds of leaving the cheetah enclosure she was in the wood on the hill crest, the first burst of fierce speed dead in her. She found a small path and moved along it, trotting now. Fear and panic were easing from her. With her fright and shock gone, she now found the strange restlessness she had known all day still with her. She gave herself over to it in a way she could never have done in the enclosure because she was at liberty.

It was less than twenty minutes before the Cheetah Warden in his Land-Rover discovered that Yarra was gone. Over his walkie-talkie set he sent out a message to his headquarters and arrangements were immediately put in hand to organize a search party. By then Yarra was well away, beyond the wood, moving slowly down the lee of a small orchard of bare apple trees. The land dropped steeply below her. A mile away she could see the line of a road with cars speeding along it.

Yarra stopped, watched the road for a while, and then turned and began to work a line across country parallel to the road below.

2

ᔆ *Shelter for Two* ᔆ

If there was an instinct in Yarra to keep away from
human beings and roads, there was the same
instinct in Smiler. Dressed now in his own clothes,
the blanket abandoned under a bush, since he knew
it was too distinguishing a mark if he should be
sighted with it, he half-walked, half-trotted along
the downlands that ran away from the wood. He kept
just below the crest of all ridges because he knew,
without having to think about it, that if he walked
the crestlines he would be too easily seen. He had
no idea where he was, not even the name of the
county, nor of the nearest town. All he had known
was that the policemen had been taking him to
Salisbury. Salisbury meant nothing to him except
that he vaguely remembered that there was a
cathedral there.

His wet jeans, although they were warming up a
bit with his body heat, rubbed him on the inside of
his thighs. His wet shirt clung to him under the
heavy, sodden weight of his jacket like a tight top
skin. He was hungry and he kept thinking of all the
second helpings he had refused in his life. Beautiful
pictures of steaming sausages and beans, hamburgers
and packets of golden potato crisps floated before
his eyes until he sternly gave himself a smart
talking-to and said, "Samuel M., keep your eyes
open for danger not for food."

He travelled for two hours across country and not for a single second did it stop raining. The thunder and lightning went gradually, sliding away into the east and finally dying out with a few muffled grumbles and a pale, distant streak of blue fire. The rain soaked into his thick tweed jacket so that it grew heavier and heavier on him. The water ran down his fair hair, plastering it to his head like thickly spread butter. It seeped down between his shirt collar and his neck and trickled over his naked body cooling down any heat his exercise was giving him. He shivered now and then. He began to feel miserable, too, but he told himself that misery was to be expected in the circumstances and the best way to beat it was to find shelter for the coming night.

He crossed three roads, one of them a main highway, hiding first in the hedges until the coast was clear and then darting across. The policemen, he knew, would have sent out a pickup call for him. The last thing he was going to have happen was to be picked up and taken back to the reform school.

Now and again he would sing quietly to cheer himself up. The songs were always ones his father had taught him, ones he had sung while his father played his mouth-organ. Sometimes when his father was home from sea they would go out on borrowed bicycles – Sister Ethel's for him and her husband's for his father – and they would freewheel down hills both of them singing madly. Once or twice his father had hired a car and taken them out. Each time, when they were on some quiet road, his father had let him drive and he had soon picked up the knack.

He was trotting up a river valley, following a small

partly overgrown path, the stream heavy with flood water to his right, when he saw ahead of him a low greystone bridge. Smiler came cautiously out on to the bridge and looked up and down the road. There was no one in sight. On the far side of the bridge, set a little back from the water's edge, was a long, low, thatched cottage. A board on the garden gate read – Ford Cottage. Farther up the road was a yard entrance. Rising above the thatch of the cottage he could see the corrugated iron roof of a barn that stood behind it.

Smiler eyed the cottage for some time. There was no smoke coming out of any of the chimneys. The curtains at all the windows were drawn. He whistled quietly, speculatively to himself for a moment and then trotted up the road to the yard entrance.

The big gate was shut and there was a padlock and chain on it. Beyond the gate was a courtyard with a well in the middle and beyond that the barn with an open bay at one end which clearly served as a garage. The back of the house showed no sign of life. For a moment or two he stood there as the rain poured down on him. He slowly licked his wet, cold lips as though the cottage were something to eat.

But Smiler was not going to be caught a second time. Things were not always as they seemed. Take that old farmer who had turned him over to the police – he could have sworn that the old man had never suspected that he had laid up each night in the warm hay of his barn – but he had known and had not let Smiler suspect it until the police car had swept into the farmyard just as he was coming out of the hen house with eggs in his hands.

So Smiler made a reconnaissance, right around the house and barn, peering through the chinks in the drawn curtains and going right into the barn and up the wooden ladder to the hay-filled loft. He noticed, too, that there were no recent car tracks on the soft mud at the entrance to the car bay. At the back of the car bay, covered by a ground-sheet, was an old bicycle.

A few minutes later Smiler was in the house. It wasn't a difficult procedure. Back in his home town there were certain boys he had mixed with who had a considerable knowledge of the ways of householders with their keys when they went away. Nearly every-one locked the front door and took the key with them, and nearly everyone locked the back door and hid the key somewhere handy where the woman or friend who came to keep an eye on things could find it. The back door key of Ford Cottage was tucked away on a low rafter that formed part of the support for the porch over the door.

The back door opened directly into a large kitchen. Smiler went in and locked the door behind him. It was a nice kitchen, though now a bit gloomy with the yellow and red curtains drawn. It had all the modern appliances, including a deep-freezer, and on one of the walls was a big picture of a group of pink flamingoes standing in shallow water.

Smiler put out a hand and flicked the light switch by the door. The centre light came on. Smiler flicked the light off. He went to the sink and turned the cold tap. Water ran from it. He turned the hot tap. No water came from it. Smiler decided that if it became necessary he would puzzle that one out later. The most pressing need at the moment was to find some food and something warm to wear.

Five minutes later Smiler was out of the cottage (the back door locked and the key returned to its place) and up in the hayloft of the barn. He had with him – found in the kitchen sideboard – two tins of sardines with keys cellotaped to them for opening, a big, unopened packet of slightly salty biscuits and a large bottle of hard cider. The whole lot he carried in a thick car rug which he had found in the little hall outside the kitchen.

Smiler picked himself a spot on the hay bales where he could lie and watch the yard through a dusty, cobwebbed little window. Methodically he stripped off his clothes, wrung them out as best he could and then spread them over the bales to dry. The red dye of his socks had run and given his feet a rosy pink hue. He wrapped himself in the thick, warm car rug. It was made of a furry kind of nylon stuff and tickled his bare skin in a pleasant kind of way.

All his dispositions made, Smiler sat down and began to attend to the inner man. Within fifteen minutes he had eaten all the sardines, and drunk the oil they were preserved in. He had worked his way through two-thirds of the packet of biscuits and had considerably punished the contents of the bottle of cider. Almost immediately he began to regret the cider because it started to make his head spin a little. He had to keep flicking his eyelids up and down to clear his vision so that he could watch the yard outside. But it was no good. Flick as he might, he could not keep his eyes from wanting to shut. There were moments, too, when his head seemed to

16

be spinning so fast that it threatened to take off like a helicopter. The last thing Smiler remembered before slumping in to sleep was giving himself a good talking-to, saying, "Samuel M., my lad, you wolfed your food and swigged your cider like a glutton. If you don't end up by being sick, it'll be a miracle."

*   *   *

While Smiler was sleeping flat out on his hay bales in the loft, and snoring so loudly that anyone who had come by the barn would have heard him, Yarra was about a mile and a half away from him on the far side of the valley through which the river by Ford Cottage ran. The rain had slackened to a thin drizzle now. Some time before, following the line of the road she had first seen, Yarra had found herself coming into an area with more and more cottages and houses. Instinctively she had turned away southwards to avoid, although she didn't know it, what were the outskirts of the town of Warminster. Her restlessness was still with her and with it now there was also another feeling. Yarra was hungry. It was between five and six o'clock in the afternoon which was past the time at which the cheetahs were normally fed. More significantly, this day was a Tuesday which meant that Yarra was hungrier than usual because in the Longleat animal reserve Monday was a fast day for all the big cats. They were given no food on that day for health reasons. In their wild state the big cats hunted and then ate, and then only hunted for food again when hunger returned. To feed them regularly every day would in the end have dulled their appetites and injured their health. So, each Monday, they were starved. Yarra now had her eyes open for the chance to find something to eat.

Moving along the grass headland at the side of a field of young winter wheat, which was bounded by a post and wire fence, Yarra caught the quick movement of something white to her left. Immediately she froze in her tracks. She remained statu-esquely still, her right foreleg poised immobile in mid-air. Beyond the low fence was a small run of pasture that sloped up to a line of tall elms. Through the trees showed a glimpse of a red-roofed house with a wisp of smoke coming from its chimneys. At the foot of the elms was a large wooden chicken-house, perched up on iron wheels so that it could be moved from one field to another. Scattered around the henhouse and out across the field was a flock of White Leghorn fowls.

Yarra watched them and rich saliva rose swiftly to her mouth. She stretched her jaws silently and then dropped low to the ground. For all her bulk Yarra moved under the bottom strand of the fence wire like a silent flow of undulating, molten, tawny gold, shadowed by the fast ripple of her markings. Once through the fence she remained for a while flat to the ground. Fifty yards away she marked the nearest straggler from the flock, a cock bird with fine rain-washed comb and wattles of shining vermilion. The great arch of its white, cockaded tail was ruffled now and again by the wind which was rising, coming in from the west to sweep away the last of the rain.

With a slow deliberate movement Yarra rose to her feet. Her eyes on the cock, she moved forward.

Her body was charged with the controlled intensity of her stalking and the sharp lust for food inside her. Every movement she made came from instinct and from hereditary memory. Although she had been captured as a well-grown cub, and had never done much hunting for herself, she moved now as surely and knowledgeably as though she had spent all her time in the wilds where she had been born.

She was twenty yards from the bird when it saw her. Its head turned with a jerk that flicked wide its cape feathers and tumbled its bold crest. At these movements Yarra streaked into action. She went fast across the winter-pale grass in two running leaps. The cock bird screamed in alarm and jumped high, wings slashing the air. Yarra took the bird three feet from the ground, her jaws closing over its lower neck, crushing and breaking the vertebrae. A great white explosion of feathers sprayed into the drizzle-soft wind. Farther across the pasture there was a noisy gust of alarm calls from the other fowls as they scooted across the grass with flapping wings for the shelter of the henhouse.

Yarra, holding her prey high, raced back to the wire fence and cleared it with an easy spring. She loped away down the far side of the field and then turned through an open gateway out on to the hummocky, steep sides of a sweep of bracken- and gorse-covered downland.

She found a hollow, ringed by gorse and broom bushes and, couching down, the cock between her outstretched paws, began to eat it. She tore and gnawed at the carcase, relishing the warm savour of its entrails and stringy flesh. She ate like a cat, seldom holding the food with her paws, but jerking, chewing and tearing at it with her strong teeth. When she had finished there were left only the wings, the once boldly arched tail and the stout yellow legs of the proud cock.

Her meal finished, Yarra groomed and cleaned herself, licking the margins of her great jaws, and carefully combing with her rasping tongue her creamy chest mantle. She lay for a while on her side, contented, her head twisted back on one shoulder, and grunted once or twice with the pleasure of the food inside her.

The rain stopped and the wind, swinging from the west to the south, strengthened and began to clear the clouds from the evening sky so that a few early stars showed thinly. Yarra rose, her old, unnameable restlessness back with her. But this time there was habit with it, too. Each night in the cheetah reserve Yarra with all the others – Lotus, Apollo, Schultz, Suki and the rest – was herded by the warden in his Land-Rover into the night pen at the bottom of the enclosure where they were shut in. In fact it was seldom necessary for them to be herded in by the warden. As darkness came habit activated them and they sought the cover of the warm, straw-floored hut of their own accord. Night was coming fast now and Yarra moved on to find a place to shelter herself.

Half an hour later, the dusk thickening, she came down a valley side and up on to a high bank above a main road. A car went by quickly with its sidelights on. Its movement did not alarm Yarra. She was used to cars and to the smell of exhaust fumes. The small lights on the car puzzled her a little but with the passing of the car her curiosity went. She dropped down the bank side on bunched feet and was across the main road like a shadow. On the far side a minor road, stone-walled and thorn- and hazel-topped, ran down towards the river. Something white in the hedge attracted Yarra's attention. It was no living thing but she padded towards it with caution, sniffed it and then passed on down the side road. The white thing was a small direction board with the words – Ford Cottage – on it, followed by a black arrow pointing down the road. Three-quarters of a mile away at that moment Smiler was sitting up in the gloom on his hay bale, groaning and holding his head, knowing that within the next few minutes he was going to be violently sick.

Yarra padded down the road, flicking a front paw now and then with irritation because the ground was running with water from the overflow of a small ditch at one side. Although it was almost dark now she could see well enough to mark the stir of a blackbird settling to roost in the mid branches of one of the hazel growths on the bank. As she neared the bottom of the lane she heard the sound of the river running in high spate. She crossed over a stone bridge, the noise of flood water loud below her. She stopped just short of the white padlocked gate which was the barn entrance to Ford Cottage.

Her eyes went over the house, cream-plastered, the old thatch grey in the dying light. Then she saw the barn across the yard with its garage bay and to the right of that an open doorway cut in the lower weather-boarding of the barn side. The doorway reminded her of the doorway at the side of her sleeping hut at Longleat. For shelter and warmth at night she knew you went through such a door. She took one long leap, went high over the five-barred gate, and landed silently in the yard and then padded forward towards the barn.

She was almost at the old wellhead in the centre of the courtyard when a figure came through the open barn door. Yarra froze. With immobility she became part of the gloom, her spotted pelt merging into the night shadows, her bulk blurring against the grey and indigo courtyard surface and the hedges and walls of her background.

The figure turned along the side of the barn with a curious stumbling and flapping movement and disappeared. Yarra knew it was a human being, the scent told her that, though it was the first time she had seen one who walked with this curious flapping movement. It was a tallish human being. The large human beings, Yarra knew, had to be treated with respect. It was the very small ones that roused her and all her kind, the children who looked through the windows of the cars going round the park. To her they were small game to be hunted, like young deer; the right size to be stalked and killed. Sometimes in the park Yarra and the other cheetahs would be suddenly and unpredictably aroused by the sight of a child and would lope alongside the car and chase it for a while. But this figure was too big to rouse any killing instinct in her.

She waited for a while to see if the figure would return. After a time, she unfroze slowly and padded across to the barn door.

*   *   *

Smiler, bare-footed, wrapped in the car rug which

flapped about his body in the strong night wind, had been sick in the little orchard that lay behind the barn. He felt better but his head still ached and his stomach was queasy and tender. Despite the blanket, he was cold, but for the moment he wasn't sure about going back to the barn. He had a feeling he might be sick again. The dizziness in his head was still there, too. That came from the cider. He'd swilled it down as though he'd been parched from thirst in a desert for weeks. He had had the same experience once before when he had gone for a day's fishing with his father. He remembered now how his father had grinned at him and said, "Samuel M., never drink too much cider under a hot sun and on an empty stomach." His father had given him black coffee from the thermos and put him to sleep in the back of the borrowed car.

Smiler walked down a small path to the edge of the river. He knelt down and splashed water over his face and head.

Five minutes later, he went back to the barn. The ladder that led to the top loft was just inside the door. Beyond the ladder the bottom floor of the barn ran back in darkness for about thirty feet. His head still dizzy and throbbing, Smiler turned through the door and groped for the ladder rungs. He was busy giving himself a good talking-to about eating and drinking like a pig. He was so busy doing this, in fact, and so full of self-pity for his queasy stomach and pounding head, that he did not hear the sudden movement of an alarmed Yarra rising to her feet on a patch of straw litter. She came up fast, dropping her shoulders, sphinx-like head thrust out, jaws open, her face-mask wrinkled with a mixture of fear and anger. She gave one sharp, spitting hiss of warning – which went unheard by Smiler as he climbed his way up the steps, grumbling aloud at the awkwardness of his blanket.

Yarra, silent now, holding her warning position, watched him go. He disappeared. There was a thump as the trapdoor at the head of the ladder was dropped.

Yarra heard noises from above. Then there was silence and she slowly relaxed. She settled again in the straw litter, flat on her side, her head thrown back at an angle from her shoulders. She was tired and she was disturbed by the restlessness in her. She could sense a slight irritation in the line of dugs along her belly. Her belly, itself, felt strange and, as she lay stretched out on her side, showed that it was slightly swollen. What Yarra didn't know, and what her Cheetah Warden at Longleat would have been delighted to know, was that she was going to have cubs. The father had been Apollo and the mating had taken place thirty days previously. In sixty days' time Yarra was due to litter. Cheetahs seldom breed in captivity and those at Longleat had never shown any signs of doing so – which was perhaps the reason why Yarra's condition, for she showed but little, had gone unnoticed.

Slowly, her restlessness fading, Yarra dropped away into sleep.

Above her, rug-wrapped in a nest of hay, Smiler slept, too, and dreamt that his father had got a job for him in his company. They had shipped to sea together and here they all were; deep in the dazzling blue of the South Seas, sitting on the foredeck, sun streaming down, and albatrosses, frigate birds and gulls thick in the sky. The off-duty crew were gathered about them as his father gave out on the mouth-organ and Smiler, strong-lunged and musical, accompanied him in their favourite song:

> "*The gallant frigate* Amphitrite, *she lay in*
> *Plymouth Sound,*
> *Blue Peter at the fore-mast head, for she was*
> *outward bound.*
> *We were waiting there for orders to send us*
> *far from home,*
> *Our orders came for Rio, and then around*
> *Cape Horn . . .*"

Smiler snored gently in his sleep. A barn owl looked down on him from a dark roof recess at the end of the loft and then took off through an eave opening on silent wing to forage. Down below Yarra slept, jerking her head now and then as a stiff stem of straw tickled her muzzle.

3

ᔆ A Door Is Closed ᔆ

Just before first light Yarra woke and left the barn
She went through the orchard and down to the rive
where she crouched at the stream-side and drank
Flicking water from her muzzle, she turned awa
and moved slowly up the narrow footpath tha
fishermen used in the trout season. A hundred yard
from Ford Cottage an unwary moorhen got up fron
a dead patch of reeds almost under Yarra's nose
She took it with one swift pounce. She carried it t
the cover of a thicket of briars and ate it.

It was over an hour later when Smiler woke. H
was warm and dry and he felt better. He lay bac
on the hay looking out of the dusty window. Ove
the top of the cottage he could see the tips of a ta
row of poplars on the far side of the river. Tw
starlings sat on the television aerial fixed to th
chimney of the cottage. Through a broken pane c
the window came the sound of sparrows quarrellin
under the barn eaves, the belling of tits from th
stark apple trees in the orchard and the distar
drone of an airplane. From its dark perch right u
in the angle of the rooftree of the barn, the ow
opened one eye briefly to observe Smiler and the
closed it again.

Smiler lay thinking. The first half hour of wakin
in the morning was his best time for thought. It wa
a time of day when things seemed to present them
selves fresh and clear. At the moment it wa

impossible for him to work out any grand plan of campaign for the future. He had to be content with a short-term view, and his short-term view was that he had to keep out of sight of people as much as possible and have a base which would give him shelter, warmth, and food and drink. Ford Cottage seemed a good base if it were empty and going to be empty for some time. That was something he had got to find out if he could. The deep-freezer and the food cupboards were well stocked as he knew. The question of making use of someone else's house and supplies didn't worry him very much. After all, he told himself, if things were the other way round and he was the bloke that owned the house and there was a young chap like himself on the run – because everyone had just got everything wrong – he wouldn't have minded a bit if that young chap had helped himself. His father often said – didn't he? – that God helped those who helped themselves but God helped those most who helped others. There was no questioning that. Thing Number One, then, was to find out if the cottage was really unoccupied and, if possible, for how long it might stay that way.

Now Smiler, when he had put his mind to it, could be extraordinarily patient and industrious about any job he undertook. If you're going to do something, then make a proper job of it, his father was always saying, because, if you don't, you'll founder in the first stiff breeze that comes along.

So, from his barn window Smiler watched the cottage all that morning. The only person who came to the house was a postman who appeared at mid-morning and pushed some letters through the back door slot. Twice a red tractor came down and back the side road, moving over the bridge and up the steep wooded rise beyond. For lunch Smiler ate all the salt biscuits that remained and drank the little cider that was left.

An hour later he had a shock. From the window he saw an elderly man come walking down the road. He wore a tweed coat and a checked cap and he stopped at the courtyard gate and looked across to the barn. Smiler saw him shake his head and then come through the wicket gate at the side of the large gate and cross to the barn. Down below Smiler heard the open barn door being banged-to on its catch. His heart beating fast, he saw with relief the man moving back across the yard to the lane. When the man was gone Smiler gave himself a black mark for carelessness. The door had originally been closed on the catch and he had left it open. The elderly man was probably some neighbour who could have fancied it had blown open in the night's wind and had taken the trouble to close it. But if he had, Smiler argued, then it probably meant that the neighbour knew there was no one in the cottage. After all, you didn't go around shutting a friend's barn door if you knew the friend would be back soon, say like that evening, or the next day.

An hour after the man had gone Smiler went out of the barn – closing the door after him. Keeping his eyes smartly open, he slipped across to the back door. He took the key and opened it. The lock was a Yale. Smiler put the key back on the porch rafter and, once in the cottage, closed the door on the free catch. He could get out from the inside by turning the latch. He went through the hall to the front door and found that the lock there was a Yale too. That was fine, because if he heard anyone coming in the back he could slip out of the front unseen.

In the kitchen he picked the mail from a wire basket that hung under the letter flap. There were two letters in white envelopes addressed to a Major H. E. Collingwood, Ford Cottage, Crockerton, Near Warminster, Wiltshire, and a picture postcard addressed to Mrs. B. Bagnall at the cottage. The picture on the card was a view of Mont Blanc across the Lake of Geneva and the message on it cheered Smiler up a lot. It read:

Dear Mrs. B.

Mrs. Collingwood and I send our regards and I am happy to say she is much improved in health though it will be a good month yet before the medico will be able – we hope – to give her a clean bill of health.

When you next come in and find this will you please check the level of the central heating oil tank as I don't trust that oil fellow to call regularly to top it up.

Kind regards to you, Mr. B., and family.

Sincerely,

H. B. Collingwood.

So, thought Smiler, the Major is away with his wife for quite a time and Mrs. Bagnall, whoever she was, came in now and then to keep an eye on things. Well, all he had to do was to keep a weather-eye open for Mrs. Bagnall. Considerably perked up, whistling gently to himself, he gave himself a good wash at the kitchen sink. He dried himself on a roller towel fixed to the back of a door next to the washing machine. Opening the door, he discovered that it held a small central heating plant. Now from Sister Ethel's Albert – who was a plumber and electrical engineer – Smiler knew quite a lot about heating plants. Albert had often taken him on jobs and was, anyway, forever talking about his work. This plant was set at 60 degrees Fahrenheit, and the time clock was adjusted so that it came on at nine o'clock at night and went off at eight in the morning . . . enough, Smiler knew, to keep the cottage warm and damp free and to avoid any danger of pipes freezing up.

Smiler put the letters and the postcard back in the mail basket and tidied up the sink from his washing. As a precaution he pulled the roller towel up so that no one could see that he had used it. He then made a quick tour of the cottage, promising himself a more detailed one later. This done, he slipped out of the back door and over to his barn, closing the door after him.

He took with him – strictly on loan – a small portable transistor set which he had found in the Major's study. The inside of his shirt was pouched with a can of corned beef, key attached for opening, a packet of Ryvita biscuits, and a bottle of orange juice. He ate and drank unhurriedly, although he was considerably sharp-set with hunger. While he ate he turned the radio on very softly.

Some time before it got really dark Smiler gathered up his empty sardine tins and the corned-beef can and the now empty packet of salt biscuits and the cider bottle. Holding the rubbish clasped to his breast he went down the ladder frontwards, without the use of his hands, bumping his bottom from rung to rung to keep his balance. At the door he jerked up the catch with one shoulder and hooked the door open with his foot. The dusk was thickening. There was no one about. He slipped out. Because he was only going to go a few yards to the river to dump his rubbish he left the door open. To close it would have meant the nuisance of putting all the tins on the ground and using his hands.

He went quickly round the corner of the barn and through the garden to the river which was still running high with the previous day's rains. He threw his load into the flood water and then bent down to wash his hands which had become sticky with sardine oil.

*　　*　　*

Yarra came wraith-like through the gloom at the top of the garden. She saw Smiler by the river, her head turning at the movement of his arm as he tossed his rubbish into the water, her nostrils catching his scent almost at the same time. She moved on without pausing and without any great interest in him. The scent was the same as she had caught the previous night, though the shape was leaner and no flapping came from it. Had she been hungry and in a bad temper just the sight of him might have stirred resentment. But she was well-fed and wanted only the comfort of her hut and the litter of warm straw. That morning she had worked her way upstream on the right bank of the river through steep plantation slopes of young firs and old woods of bare trees. She had taken a grey squirrel – tempted out by the sunshine – as it had scurried for the trunk of a tall beech, jumping and pawing it down from the smooth grey bark when it was six feet from the ground. Full of her waterhen meal, she had done no more than take a bite from its soft belly and leave it. Most of the day she had passed in the river woods, moving away whenever she had heard voices or sounds that disturbed her. During the late afternoon she had come out of the woods at the top of the river slope. Here, on a long, rolling down, she had put up a hare from a clump of dead bracken. Yarra had seen hares before moving across the parkland pasture outside her Longleat enclosure. They had always excited her just as did the young deer that also moved beyond the wire in freedom. She had gone after the hare, hearing the thump of its feet as it raced away. The hare had had a fifteen-yard start on her but, although it had twisted, zig-zagged and doubled at top speed, she had moved like an orange-gold blur and taken it within a hundred yards easily. She had eaten it, relishing the meat which was strange to her.

Now, full of food, wanting only her resting place, she passed around the barn and through the open door to find her litter of straw. In the darkness she pawed with her claws at the flattened straw to shape and bulk it. Satisfied after a while, she dropped flat on it. She stretched her legs stiffly, tightened her shoulder muscles, and then relaxed, her head cocked over one shoulder watching the open doorway.

A few moments later Smiler came through the door, humming softly to himself. Momentarily Yarra's mask wrinkled and she opened her jaws, half-threatening, but making no sound. There was no real malice in her.

Smiler closed the door on the latch, felt for the

ladder rungs in the darkness and went up to his loft and dropped the trapdoor quietly.

* * *

That evening before going to sleep Smiler listened to the radio for two or three hours. He had the set turned down very low and tucked into the hay close to his head. When the news came on he was interested to hear whether there would be anything about his escape on it. But he was disappointed. It would have been quite something to have had his own name broadcast.

However, there was something about another escaper. A cheetah (Smiler tried to picture what a cheetah was like and fancied it was something like a panther or leopard) which had escaped from the Longleat wild life reserve the day before had not so far been found. Smiler – whose home was at Fishponds on the outskirts of Bristol – had heard of Longleat and its lions though he had never been there. No one had yet reported seeing the animal but the Longleat authorities had said that it was not likely to travel far. It was probably still quite close to the park or somewhere in the large tract of country in the triangle made by the towns of Frome, Warminster and Mere. Anyone seeing the animal was asked to keep well away from it and to inform the police or the Longleat Park authorities. At the end of the news there was a short interview with a man from Longleat Park who gave some general information about cheetahs. In the course of it he said that the name of the escaped cheetah was Yarra and that it was a female.

Before sleeping Smiler lay comfortably in the hay thinking about the cheetah. He'd often gone to the Bristol Zoo but he couldn't remember whether he had ever seen a cheetah there. Actually he didn't care much for zoos. Having animals in big parks like Longleat was much better. Pacing up and down a cage was no way to live. Being at a reform school – although he hadn't stayed there long – was a bit like that. Do this, do that, and being watched all the time, feeling and knowing every moment that you were a prisoner. Even having a big enclosure to live in wasn't really good enough, he felt. Not if you were a wild animal. All right for cows and sheep. But not for a leopard or a lion or a cheetah. Yarra . . . that was a nice name . . . same sort of name in a way as Tarzan. Yarra and Tarzan. He saw himself in a loin cloth swinging through the jungle trees. His faithful cheetah, Yarra, followed him far below, looking up when he gave his jungle cry. He liked animals, though he had never had many. The best had been a mongrel dog, black with white patches and a head that had a bit of Alsatian in it, called Tessa. His father had brought it home for him one day. Tessa would do anything for him. When he went to stay with Sister Ethel, while his father was at sea, she had made a terrible fuss. Tessa's hairs got all over the furniture and carpets. In the end, he was sure, Tessa had got fed-up with all the fuss, too, because one day while he was walking her on the downs she had gone off and never come back . . . Tessa . . . Yarra . . . and Tarzan. He yawned, switched the radio off and stretched out to go to sleep.

*　　*　　*

34

So far Smiler and Yarra had been lucky. No one had sighted either of them. Two of the wardens from Longleat had tried to follow Yarra's spoor marks from the point of her breakout. After a time they had to give it up because the rain had washed them away. Nobody had tried to follow Smiler's tracks. The police had sent out their signals and had alerted all patrol cars and the local constabulary with a description of Smiler. Now they were pretty confident that the need for food or shelter would make Smiler show up somewhere pretty soon. It was no time of the year for living rough, particularly as Smiler was far from being a country boy. The police had, of course, got in touch with Sister Ethel, giving her the news, and telling her that if Smiler appeared she must report him at once.

Ethel and her husband, Albert, were at this moment in the sitting room of their little villa in Fishponds having cocoa before going to bed. It was a small neat room, everything shining and brushed, and polished and dusted. Albert had his slippers on. He was never allowed in the room without them. Albert was much easier going than Ethel, though he would never have dared to break any of her rules in the house. He was master only in his own workshop.

Ethel said, "That boy's always been a trouble and always will be. He's got a wild, stubborn streak in him – and I wouldn't know where it came from."

Albert knew that everybody had streaks of some kind in them. You just had to make the most of the streak you were handed out with, as – he had no doubt – Smiler would do with his one day. He liked Smiler.

He said, "My opinion is he run away from that

place because he knew he didn't ought to have been there in the first instance."

Ethel put her cocoa mug down precisely in the middle of a little table mat and said, "He went there because he was a bad one. Knocking an old lady over and taking her bag. And before that always lifting and taking things. Bad company makes bad habits."

Albert sighed gently. "He was light-fingered, yes. But I'm not sure he was any more than that. Not violent. Not Smiler. He wouldn't harm a fly, let alone an old lady. All right, at the time it looked black against him and I thought he had done it. But now, on due and full consideration, I don't think he did. Not Smiler."

"He was always nicking things and getting into scrapes. The way you start is the way you go on, and you go on nicking bigger things and getting into bigger scrapes. And that's what happened. Although he's my own brother, I have to say it."

Albert put his mug down on the polished table top, discovered his mistake and moved it to his little table mat, and said reflectively, "It's all a matter of what they call psychology."

"Whatever are you talking about?"

"Psychology. How the mind works. Smiler was what they call compensating for his home life – or rather for the home life he wasn't getting. No mother and his dad off to sea nine months out of twelve and only us to come to when he was on his own –"

"And what's wrong with us? We give him as good a home as anyone could."

"That's just it. As good as we could. But it

36

weren't good enough, Ethel. He never knew his Mum and he missed his Dad. We couldn't do anything about that. But he, unconsciously, you understand, tried to. That's why he went out and about nicking things and getting into scrapes. He was what they call making his protest against what society was doing to him."

Ethel sniffed loudly. "Well, I must say, that's the fanciest notion I've ever heard. And anyway, conscious or unconscious, he did that old lady and she stood right up in the juvenile court and identified him."

Albert rose. His cocoa was finished and now he meant to go out to his workshop and smoke his goodnight cigarette. He liked to sit on his bench and puff away while he dreamed impossible dreams – sometimes like being able to smoke in the parlour and the bedroom, to flick ash on the floor, to put his feet up on anything he chose and, perhaps now and then, to have a bottle of beer instead of cocoa for a bedtime drink.

He said pungently: "That old lady was as blind as a bat! She couldn't have recognized her own reflection in a mirror! And I don't believe she ever had twenty pounds in her handbag. Smiler had only ten on him when they nabbed him five minutes later." He moved to the door and added, "Well, I hope the lad's found a fair billet for tonight. It's freezing out."

"That poor boy," said Ethel. "His father'll raise the roof when he comes home."

"When," said Albert and went out.

*   *   *

Albert was right. It was freezing. It froze hard all night. When the first light began to come up over the easterly ridge of the river valley it was to reveal a world laced and festooned with a delicate tracery of frost. The frost ribboned the bare trees and hung from the thin branches in loops and spangles. It had carpeted the grass with a crisp layer of brittle icing, and had frozen the water splashings under the old stone bridge so that they hung in fanglike stalactites, and had coated the small pools and puddles with a black sheeting of ice. It was a rime- and hoar- and ice-covered world made suddenly dazzlingly beautiful as the first lip of the sun showed to strike gleams of white, gold and blue fire from every branch and twig and every hanging icicle.

The brightening crack of light under the barn door woke Yarra. She rolled over and sat up on her haunches. She tightened the muscles of her long forelegs to ease the night's laziness from them. She sat, sphinx-fashion in the gloom like an ancient Egyptian cat goddess, her liquid amber eyes watching the light under the door. Although the door was closed, and had not been the previous night, it did not seem strange to her. The door of her hut at Longleat was always closed during the night and the warden opened it early in the morning. She sat waiting for the sound of his feet outside. Sometimes he was early and sometimes late.

Half an hour passed and the warden did not come. Yarra rose to her four feet, walked to the door and sniffed at it. Then she turned back along the far wall. Her restlessness was coming back fast. She walked back to her straw, scraped at it, working her shoulder muscles, and then went to the door again. She wanted to be outside, where the world was full of sounds, blackbirds and sparrows calling, the beat of a car's engine passing down the narrow road and the low, mocking caws of rooks moving from their night roosts to forage on the iron-hard field furrows.

Annoyed now, she raised herself on her hind feet and scraped against the shut door, rattling and banging it impatiently.

The scraping, rattling and banging from down below eventually woke Smiler. He lay on his hay bed, still a little muzzy with sleep, listening to it. It took him a minute or two to remember where he was. When he did, he jumped quickly to his feet and stood above the trapdoor. Somebody was down below! With the thought his heart began to thump with alarm. He knelt down and cautiously lifted the lid of the loft trap an inch and peered through. His eyes, dazed from the sunlight which was streaming in through his loft window, could make out nothing in the gloom below. Then, as his eyes slowly adjusted themselves, he saw the movement at the barn door. For a moment or two he watched, his mouth open in amazement. Then – with a swift, panic reaction – he dropped the trapdoor and shot across the holding bolt which was fastened to the top of it. He dropped back to a sitting position on the hay, clapped a hand to his forehead, and said out loud, "Blimey O'Bloody Reilly!"

4

⌐ A Door Is Opened ⌐

As Smiler sat there considering the situation the skin of his scalp crept with a slow shiver of fear as he realized what a narrow escape he had had. Not this morning – but last night! When he had come back from throwing the rubbish away he had closed the barn door and *that thing* had already been in the barn! He had closed the door and climbed the ladder and *that thing* must have been watching him! And now *that thing* was down there and he was up here!

What on earth was he going to do? To help his thoughts he swigged off what remained of the orange juice. Then, because no helpful thoughts came, he drew back the bolt of the loft trap and raised it a few inches cautiously. Down below Yarra was padding restlessly up and down. She caught the slight movement of the loft trap out of the corner of her eye and swung round. She backed away a little, raised her head, and made an angry movement of her jaws.

Smiler could see her clearly now. He saw the wrinkling of her face mask, the white shine of her teeth, the restless switching of the long tail, the tensing of the high powerful shoulders, and the long, lean length of her forelegs and body. He dropped the loft trap back into place and bolted it.

Smiler was no fool. He could put two and two together faster than many young lads. "Samuel M.," he said to himself, the problem on his hands now overcoming his shock and fright, "what you have got down there is that escaped cheetah! Yarra. That's right. And what you are stuck with right now is that you can't get out until you get her out. That's Thing Number One without any question."

He got up and went to the barn window, scratching his head. He looked out. It was still very early in the morning. The sun was only just half clear of the valley ridge. He took a good look at the window for the first time, and he saw that it was not fixed in its frame. There was a hook catch at one side. He pushed this up, opened the window and looked out. Six feet below him and a little to his left was the top of the barn door. Two-thirds of the way up the door and on the side closest to him was the door latch. It was a curved handgrip with a thumb press latch above it that had to be pushed down to lift the small cross lever on the inside of the door free from its notch so that the door would swing open. The door, he remembered, was awkwardly hung. Once the catch was free the door would swing inwards of its own weight.

With his head stuck out of the window he considered his plan of campaign. The window was big enough for him to get through. He could hang on to the sill and drop to the ground. It was a fair drop but not so far that it worried him. Once in the yard all he had to do was. . . . Well, what? Press the thumb latch down, give the door a push and then run for his life while that animal came through the opening after him like a streak of gold light? Not so-and-so likely he told himself. All right then, what? Just drop to the ground, and then go off and tell the police or someone that he had found the cheetah and it was shut up in the barn? Not so-and-so likely! He'd never get away with that one. It would be giving himself up and they'd have him back in reform school before you could say knife. No – there was only one way. He had to get the door open from up here and let Yarra go off on her own. Then, when she was well away, he could go down himself.

He turned back into the loft. What he wanted was a long stick with which to reach down and press the thumb catch. The loft ran well back beyond the bales of hay he had been using for a bed. When he had first come up he had made a careful inspection of the place. At the back of the loft he found a long-handled hayfork with the head broken off. It was about four feet long and would not reach the door. But in one of the corners of the loft he found a disused hutch for hens. The floor was made of long narrow strips of wood. Smiler pulled one of the slats free. Because he enjoyed problems like this, he was soon all set to try to open the door. The hay bales were all bound by lengths of binder twine. He took a couple of lengths of twine from the hay bales and lashed the hutch slat to the end of the broken hayfork. He had no trouble with making a proper lashing. His father, though a ship's cook, was also a seaman and Smiler had had a thorough grounding in tying knots. He spliced the two lengths of wood together, finishing off the whip-binding, neat and tight, so that he had a firm join. The rest was easy.

He took another look down through the loft trap at Yarra just in time to see her raise herself against the door and begin to tear at it with her forepaws

She saw his face through the hatch and turned at once and came in a swift bound to the foot of the ladder.

Smiler dropped the hatch with a bang and shot the bolt across. He went to the window quickly. Yarra was getting angry at being shut in. He pushed his home-made pole through the window and after a couple of attempts managed to bang down the thumb catch. The door slowly began to swing open.

Before he could get his pole back through the window Yarra was out. She came out slowly, stopped a yard from the open door, and then looked up at Smiler. She gave him a quick snapping hiss and then loped away around the corner of the barn. Seeing her only for a few moments in the full sunlight, Smiler was awed by her beauty. Her picture remained in his mind long after she was gone. He only had to shut his eyes and he could see the tawny gold pelt with its close-spaced black spots, the blunt, short-eared head with the long bracketing black face markings, the amber eyes and the graceful droop and upturned tuft of her tail and, most of all, the slow muscle flow of shoulders and haunches as she moved away.

*   *   *

Yarra passed that day in the same area. The restlessness in her she was used to now and, since she had her freedom, the habit was strong in her to want to come back to her barn shelter at night.

She went up the river and stopped to drink just above the barn where a small carrier stream came into the main stream over a low waterfall. In the woods higher up the river she marked the movement of a cock pheasant foraging among the dead leaves. She covered twenty yards of ground before the bird saw her. It took off too late and was brought down in a burst of feathers by one sweep of her taloned right forepaw. She ate. While she did so she heard the sound of children laughing and playing away across the river, heard the whine of cars on the not too distant main road running from Warminster down to Mere. She was outside, by at least a mile, of the triangle of roads joining Frome, Warminster and Mere. That afternoon, late, she ran down another hare on the downland above the river woods.

The frost had held all day and as the winter sun began to drop and the air turned even colder Yarra came off the downland. She was passing through a thicket of trees, studded here and there by tall, rank growths of wild rhododendrons, when a keeper, shotgun under his arm, stepped out on to the path ten yards ahead. Man and beast saw each other at the same time. Startled, Yarra backed away, lowering head and shoulders threateningly, and gave a slow snarl. The keeper, seeing her threatening stance, acted instinctively. He swung his shotgun to his shoulder and fired.

The swift movement of the gun, although she had never been fired at before, was warning enough for Yarra. Sudden movement marked something you either hunted or avoided. This was a large human, not something she hunted. She leaped sidewards into the cover of a patch of young birch. The keeper fired, first one barrel and then the other as Yarra disappeared into the gloom of the birches. The gunshots echoed through the wood. A few pellets from the spread of shot that rattled against tree trunks and the hard ground caught Yarra on the left flank, stinging and biting into her. Then she was gone at top speed through the woods.

The keeper stood in the centre of the path trembling with shock. No fool, he began to move quickly back up the path towards the open fields at the top of the wood. The wood was no place to stay in with an animal like a cheetah about. Recognition had come to him only after he had impulsively fired. Ten minutes later he was telephoning from his cottage to the Warminster police station.

* * *

That morning, after Yarra had gone, Smiler stayed in the loft. He waited patiently to see if the postman was going to call or perhaps Mrs. Bagnall, come to do some morning housework in the cottage. Eventually he saw the postman ride by the cottage on his bicycle, but he did not deliver any letters.

An hour later Smiler was in the cottage, the back door locked with the key on the outside so that he would have warning if anyone came. He had a drink of water from the tap, sluiced himself for toilet over head and neck, and then opened a tin of baked beans and ate them with a spoon from the can. He tidied up meticulously and then started another inspection of the house.

The hallway running to the front door was red carpeted and hung with small, coloured pictures of birds and flowers. There was a big oak chest in it with a wide shallow glass bowl on top. The bowl was full of odds and ends. On either side of the hall were a dining-room and a large sitting-room, one wall of which was covered entirely with bookshelves. In the window stood a flat-topped desk. Its surface was inlaid with red morocco leather and tooled around the edges in gold-leafed designs. It was as nice a room as Smiler had ever been in in his life. The chairs and settees were comfortable and well-worn. He was sure there would be no fuss if you put your feet up on them.

On the top floor, which you went up to by way of an open staircase with roughly carved bannisters and supports, were three bedrooms. One was large with two beds in it. The others had a single bed each. Leading off the big bedroom was a bathroom. The bathroom, wide and spacious, had a long window that looked out over the well-yard at the back. The bath was blue and tiled on two sides. Each tile had a picture of a fish on it. Smiler had never seen a bathroom like it, and it had a nice scented smell which he liked. If it had been his Sister Ethel's, he thought, no one would have been allowed in it without having a bath first. He poked about in it for a while and opened a mirror-fronted cabinet that hung on the wall. There were lots of bottles, tubes, toothbrushes, packets and sprays and pill boxes in the cabinet. When Smiler closed the cabinet his reflection confronted him in the mirror, snub-nosed, blue-eyed, freckles all over his face like the markings on a skylark's egg, and his blond hair tousled all over his head. He took a comb from the shelf under the cabinet, wetted it under the cold tap, and tidied his hair.

Then he went down to the sitting-room and looked at the books on the shelves. Smiler liked books.

Although he preferred adventure stories, strip comics and do-it-yourself books, he would read anything even if he didn't understand half of it. At Fishponds, if it were raining or he felt bored or he didn't want for a while to be with the other lads, he would often go into the Public Library and sit over a book in the Reading Room. The woman who ran the place was a bit sniffy with him at first but she had got to know him and, providing his hands were clean, she let him stay as long as he liked.

There were hundreds of books on the cottage shelves, a lot of them about fishing and hunting, rows of novels, a pile of Ordnance Survey maps at the end of one shelf, and on the bottom shelf a row of the Encyclopaedia Britannica. Smiler knew all about the encyclopaedia. His father had once told him that you could find out about everything in it. And it was true, as Smiler had more than once proved in the Reading Room.

For two hours Smiler sat on the floor enjoying himself. Although the curtains were drawn plenty of sunlight filtered through. Because of the central heating which had been on all night, it was not cold. He looked up all about cheetahs in the encyclopaedia. Not that there was much about them, just twenty lines or so. Smiler was interested to read that, for centuries in Persia and India, cheetahs had been used for hunting small game and antelopes. They were hooded, then taken out, and, when the hood was slipped, away they went after whatever it was. He remembered Yarra coming out of the barn. Yarra and Tarzan. Yarra and Samuel M. . . . He lay back on the floor, saw himself with a cheetah on the leash, the cheetah hooded, and the two of them moving along a great hillside then . . . Wheeeh! Off came the hood, the leash was slipped, and Yarra was away after a deer!

He sat up and grinned to himself. Some hope, Samuel M., he thought. Anyway that cheetah was miles away by now if it had any sense. He pushed the book back on to the lower shelf. As he did so he saw that at the end of the shelf, wedged between the last volume and the wooden upright, was a large glass bottle. Smiler recognized it at once. His Dad liked his whisky at night and had had bottles like this. It was a dimple-sided whisky bottle. In the top was a home-made cork with a slit cut in it that you could drop money through. The bottle was three-quarters full of sixpenny pieces. Smiler picked it up. It weighed like a bomb. He shook it, and then wondered how much there would be in it. . . . Pounds and pounds. Ten at least.

As he put the bottle back he suddenly heard a key scraping at the back door lock. Smiler was up and into the hall and out of the front door like a shot. He ran across the garden away from the road and bridge. He raced up the hillside and turned into a small clump of stunted yews. From here he could look down on the cottage and barn.

Although he couldn't see all the courtyard at the back, he could see the big white gate at the entrance. While he watched he was pleased to think that he had not left any tell-tale traces in the house. He was on the run and could not afford to give himself away. The whisky bottle was back in its place, and all the books. And he had tidied up the kitchen, wiping the sink fairly dry from his washing, putting the spoon away in its drawer, and dropping the empty baked-bean tin in the waste bin. If his Sister Ethel could have known how tidy he had been she would have thought he was sickening for something or working up to some outrageous request to be allowed to do something she would normally have refused. Then he began to worry about the baked-bean tin. Whoever had gone in might look in the bin and see it. That would give the game away. Or say they knew exactly what had been in the cupboards and spotted how he had helped himself? Well, there was nothing he could do about it now.

After about five minutes Smiler saw a woman come across the little bit of the yard he could see. She had a blue woollen hat on and a thick brown coat, and she wheeled a bicycle with a black shopping bag hanging from the handlebars. She was dumpy-looking and oldish. She pushed her bicycle through the side wicket gate and then rode away over the river bridge and up the slope beyond.

Smiler gave her a few minutes to get clear and then he began to move back. But he did not go to the cottage. He went along the hillside through the trees and dropped down into the side road. He walked down the hill, looking as though he were out for a stroll, past the big white gate and on to the bridge. Here he leaned over the parapet and pretended to be looking at the river. But his eyes were on the house and the front door, and the curtained windows. For all he knew more than one person might have gone into the house and only the woman had come out. It proved a very wise precaution. He had hardly been there a few minutes when the front door opened and a girl came out. She slammed the door to lock behind her, and then came across the lawn, out on to the road, and towards Smiler who was still hanging over the bridge parapet.

She was a nice-looking girl – with a tanned complexion and shoulder-length black hair – wearing a shiny red plastic coat and high black boots. Back in Fishponds there had been plenty of girls who hung about with Smiler's friends. Smiler didn't dislike girls, but he hadn't got a lot of time for most of them. They never seemed to say or do anything that was particularly interesting. Just laughed and giggled most of the time, or talked about clothes and a lot of nonsense.

As the girl came on to the bridge she saw Smiler. Smiler stared down at the river and hoped she would pass on. She didn't. She stopped behind him and said, "Hullo."

Smiler half-turned. "Hullo," he said.

"What are you doing here?"

"Just looking at the river," said Smiler. She seemed all right. She had a friendly smile and it suddenly occurred to him that he might get some useful information from her. He nodded his head at the cottage. "You live there?"

"No. My mum does for them. Once a week. I just come down with her."

"She the one that went up on the bike?"

" 'Sright."

"Whyn't you go back with her?"

The girl laughed. It was a nice laugh and her teeth showed very white against her tanned face. "You're a one for questions, aren't you?"

"Sorry. I was just asking."

"Well, I comes down with her on the back of her bike. But as it's all uphill going back . . . well, I walk. She came down to pick up the letters, but I stopped to dust the dining-room."

"Don't nobody live there, then?"

"They're away. I haven't seen you around before, have I?" The girl leaned over the parapet a yard from him.

"No."

"Where you from, then?"

For a moment Smiler hesitated and then he said, "Oh, over Warminster way." To forestall further questions along that line, he went on, "Where do you live?"

"Up the hill. 'Bout a mile. Lodge Cottage. You know it?"

"No."

The girl, who clearly had time on her hands and, like all girls, welcomed a chat – which didn't surprise Smiler – picked a lump of moss from one of the bridge stones and dropped it into the river, saying, "She's going down fast."

Puzzled, Smiler said, "Who is?"

"The river, of course. After all that rain. She's going down."

"Plenty of fish in there, I suppose?"

"Trout and grayling. My father's the water keeper. There's big trout under this bridge. Over three pound some. What's your name?"

Feeling easier in himself and now alert to gain any advantage that would help him, Smiler said, "Johnny. Johnny Pickering." Johnny Pickering was a boy that Smiler knew but didn't like. "What's yours?"

"Ivy, but I don't like it much. All my friends call me Pat."

"I like Pat best, too. How often do you and your mother come down here?"

"Once a week. Every Wednesday, mostly. But I don't always come. See that –" She suddenly nodded downstream.

Smiler followed her indication just in time to see a blue streak of fire flash across the water and disappear round a bend lower down. He said, "That's a kingfisher. I know that. Seen them when I been fishing with my Dad."

"My Dad don't like 'em. They eat the young trout." She straightened up and gave him a bright smile. "Well, I got to go. But if you live in Warminster I might see you sometime. I'm starting a job there next week. In Woolworth's. Bye."

"Bye."

She walked away up the hillroad and just before she turned a corner she looked back and gave him a wave of her arm. As girls went, Smiler thought, she wasn't too bad, and she hadn't got her face all plastered with lipstick and eyeshadow and stuff.

He waited another ten minutes and then slipped into the courtyard to the back door. Mrs. Bagnall, for he had no doubt about that now, had left the key on the rafter. He went in, leaving the key outside as usual.

The letters had gone from the basket behind the door. His baked-bean tin was still in the waste bin under the sink. He put it in his pocket. Then he took another tin of sardines from the cupboard, some frozen bread rolls from the deep-freezer and went back into the barn loft, carefully shutting the barn door after him.

He put the rolls in the sunshine on the window sill to thaw out, and then lay back on his hay and decided that he had to do some serious thinking. It was now very clear to him that his plan of campaign was not good enough.

No, Samuel M., he told himself, it just was not good enough. What he was doing was living from day to day and from hand to mouth. Also, he was living in dangerous territory where he could easily make some silly slip-up that would give him away . . . like that baked-bean tin, for instance. Mrs. Bagnall could easily have looked in the waste bin and found it. Then the fat would have been in the fire. Or she might just as easily have spotted that the sink, although he'd wiped it over with a dishcloth, wasn't really dry. Or even that the dishcloth – which ought to have been dry – wasn't. And all this food that he was nicking! . . . Mrs. Bagnall might spot things gone. . . . No, he had to make himself really safe. Not just for a few days. That was no good. He had to keep away from trouble until his father got back and sorted things out. Nobody else could, because nobody else was going to believe him about that old lady's handbag. . . . That old geezer in the juvenile court, when he'd tried to tell the truth, had just looked over his glasses, made a sour face, and grunted.

He lay back and stared at the barn rafters and began to think it out. It was hard work because almost at once problems began to come up. By the time he had worried *them* out they had given birth to other problems. It was nine months before his father would be back, maybe a year, and he had to keep from being caught all that time. . . . And, what's more – he was going to keep from being caught!

Sustained thought was hard, fatiguing work. The hay was warm and soft. After about two hours – with a break to eat sardines and half-thawed bread rolls – Smiler dropped off to sleep.

*   *   *

After being shot at by the keeper, Yarra kept moving fast. She was angry and disturbed; but the few small shot which had caught her left flank had caused no real harm to her. Her pelt was rough and wiry, without the natural sleekness of most felines, and not more than two or three pellets had penetrated her skin. The line she took across country was along the valley side, well above the river. At one place she dropped down the ivy-coated bank of the small road that led down to Ford Cottage and crossed into a plantation of young conifers. She moved diagonally down through the young trees until she reached their boundary. Below her the ground fell sharply away to the river.

She sat on her haunches looking down into the valley. It was growing darker every moment now. Up the river, away to her left was the bridge and the grey roof thatch and white-plastered end-wall of Ford Cottage. Beyond it the bulk of the barn roof showed against the darkening sky. Away to her right, farther downstream and towards the north and Warminster, she could see the lights of houses and cottages. Sometimes the movement of car headlights swept along the main road.

After a time she dropped down to the river,

found the fishing path and walked slowly upstream toward the stone bridge. She came out on to the road at the bridge side, crossed, and leapt the big white gate. She moved like a shadow close to the cottage and then across to the barn door. It was shut.

She sniffed around its lower edges for a moment. Then she leaned against it with the left side of her body, not to try to open it, but to rub her flank against it and ease the slight irritation of the gun shots in her skin. That the door should be shut she could not understand. Always the hut door was open at night in Longleat Park for the entry of the cheetahs. This was now her hut. The door should be open. She lazily stretched her jaws and gave a low, protesting rumble from her throat. Then she padded the length of the barn and moved around the open car bay. It smelled of oil and petrol and she wrinkled her nostrils in displeasure. She knew the smell and did not like it. Sometimes in high summer, when the cheetah enclosure was packed with parked and slowly moving cars, the same smell got so strong that she with the other cheetahs would move away upwind in the enclosure to avoid it.

She moved back to the barn door and raised herself against it, drawing the talons of her left forepaw in a great rasp down the rough wood surface. The movement shook the door and made it rattle on its hinges.

Up above in the loft the noise came faintly through to the sleeping Smiler.

Yarra rasped at the door again, more vigorously, rattling and shaking it. When it did not open she snarled and spat angrily.

The noise this time came clearly through to

Smiler. He came out of sleep with a start just in time to hear Yarra rattle the door again.

Heart thumping, sure that someone was coming to take him, his brain still fuddled with sleep, he was on his feet quickly and at the window. At that moment Yarra moved back, squatted on the ground, and sat staring at the door. Smiler saw her clearly.

His eyes wide with surprise, for in mulling over his plan of campaign all thought of Yarra had gone from him, he clapped his hand to his forehead and cried, "Cor, Blimey O'Bloody Reilly – she's back again!"

5

∽ A Change of Colour and Name ∽

There was no doubt in Smiler's mind of what he must do. Although he hadn't thought about Yarra much in the course of the day, he instinctively accepted that, since she was a fugitive like himself, he could not refuse her shelter. They were both in the same boat.

He got his home-made pole and opened the barn window. It was getting darker every minute now. Yarra heard him and saw the movement of the window. She backed away a few yards and raised her blunt head, stretching her jaws wide, and giving a low rumble. She knew this human being now and so far he had presented no threat.

Smiler, pushing the pole through the window, murmured, "All right, old girl. Won't take a moment."

He jabbed down in the gloom at the barn door latch. After a few tries, he hit the thumb press and the door swung back slowly. He pulled the pole back through the window and watched Yarra. The tension went from her. She padded in a small semi-circle around the open door, looked up at him once, and then moved slowly into the barn.

Smiler closed the window and then went to the trap in the loft floor and listened. He could hear the restless movements of Yarra scraping and shaping her straw and then a heavy thump as she dropped to her bed.

Well, that was all right, thought Smiler. She was all comfy for the night. She would be gone just after first light in the morning and he could go down and close the door. However, right now, he took the precaution of shooting the bolt across the trap door.

He went back to his own bed and turned the radio on softly. An hour later the news came on. The local news was given before the national news. The local, South of England news made no mention of one Samuel Miles, but it had plenty to say about Yarra, the cheetah, who was sleeping a few feet below him. The public were warned that she had been sighted that day a couple of miles from the village of Crockerton in the valley of the River Wylye. It was felt that she was still in the area and people were warned to watch out for her. She would be dangerous only if cornered or suddenly surprised. She was most likely to be dangerous to young children and parents were warned not to let them move about unaccompanied. Everyone was warned that it was unwise to walk alone in lonely woods and remote areas. A cordon was being thrown around the area of the river valley where Yarra had been sighted. It was confidently expected that she would soon be captured. Then there was an interview with the Cheetah Warden from Longleat Park, who was asked some questions about cheetahs, their habits and what they ate, and how dangerous they really were, and so on. Smiler chuckled to himself through all this. Yarra was in the news, and she was just below him.

But after the news was over, Smiler got a bit worried. Yarra was no trouble to him, and it didn't worry him that she might go about taking a few

chickens . . . but she was dangerous to small children!
Well, oughtn't he to do something about it?
Oughtn't he to drop out of the barn window now
and go and find the nearest policeman so that
Yarra could be caught?

And if he did?

Well, Samuel M., he told himself, that would be
the end of you. They would all think you were a
good lad and had done the right thing. They'd
probably interview you on television and radio –
but in the end you'd be shipped back to that school.

It was a difficult problem. Yarra would go off
tomorrow and almost certainly she would be caught
– and he would still be free. Anyway, he wasn't too
keen about dropping out of that window right now,
landing with a thump on the gravel, and having
Yarra, maybe, come out after him like a streak of
greased lightning. That wouldn't do anyone any
good, particularly Samuel M. But if Yarra weren't
caught tomorrow? Then she would come padding
back here to her shelter. Well, that one wasn't
difficult to work out. Tomorrow evening he would
leave the barn door open and he would stay in the
cottage. He could watch the barn from the bathroom
window. The moment he saw Yarra come back he
would go out through the front door and up to the
village of Crockerton. Bound to be a public telephone
box there. He could call the police, say where
Yarra was, refuse to say who he was – and then he
would have to take off smartly.

Down below him, he heard Yarra stir on her
straw, and he said aloud, "Old girl – if you got any
sense you won't come back tomorrow. And I hope
you don't, because I don't want to lose a soft billet."

59

He dropped off to sleep, thinking that it was hard that on top of his own problems he had the problem of the right thing to do about Yarra.

*　　*　　*

The sun was well up over the valley ridge when Smiler woke. The owl was back on its king post roost after a night's hunting. On the floor below the post were two or three fresh pellets which the bird had spewed up, little wet balls of fragile mouse and shrew bones, fur, and feathers from a wren that it had taken at the first paling of morning light. Smiler stretched and yawned. He had a busy day ahead of him, and maybe a dangerous one. He had his own problem to deal with and he meant to tackle it properly. No half measures. He lay for a moment, going over it in his mind, and then suddenly remembered Yarra.

He got up, unbolted the trap and looked down. The lower part of the barn was empty. Yarra had gone.

Smiler went down, peered cautiously around the corner of the open barn door to make sure that the coast was clear and then, closing the barn door, he went across to the cottage.

He went into the kitchen, had a drink of water and some biscuits and then washed his hands. There was no point in having a good wash yet, he thought.

Although he had bad habits – like smoking an occasional cigarette – and was no respecter of small items of other people's property when he was bored and idle and needed some excitement to make the day shine a little, Smiler was fundamentally a good sort. When he wished, he could be methodical, industrious and reasonably honest. In addition he was intelligent and a quick learner. He was also shrewd and far-thinking in an emergency; and he was in an emergency now. The emergency of keeping Samuel M. out of the hands of the police and all the other busybodies who wanted him to go back to that school. No thank you. Not for Samuel M. He was going to stay free until his father came back and sorted things out. . . .

After giving *his* problem much thought the previous day he had come to the following very clear conclusions:

1. He couldn't hang around Ford Cottage and the barn for nine months, cadging food and shelter.

2. So long as Major Collingwood was away, however, he could just use the barn for a sleeping place.

3. He had to find out exactly where he was (somewhere near Warminster was all he knew), and he had to go out and get a job so that he would have money for food and other things.

4. But to get a job wasn't all that easy, because the moment he showed his face anywhere some policeman with a long memory would recognize his fair hair and freckled face. He had, therefore, to disguise himself somehow – though there wasn't anything he could do about the freckles! But he could do something about his hair and about his clothes.

5. As for the job, well, he was strong and handy

and people were always advertising for help around the place. He would have to get a newspaper and see what was going.

6. And, to do all this – because people were always full of questions – he had to have answers as to who he was, where he lived, and so on and so on. For public purposes Samuel M. would have to go and a new lad take his place.

7. And if he stuck it out and wasn't caught, then some time he would have to telephone the shipping company offices in Bristol and find out what date his father was due back so that he could meet him.

It was a long list but Smiler felt that he had worked out the answers to most of the immediate problems, and he now set about them with a will. If there was something to be done he liked to get on with it.

He went first into the sitting-room and from the dimpled whisky bottle he shook out two pounds' worth of sixpenny pieces and wrapped them in his handkerchief. Then he went through the pile of Ordnance Survey maps and, after some time, found the one he wanted. It was Sheet 166 and on the red cover the town of Warminster was marked with a lot of others. Smiler liked and knew about maps. When he and his father had gone off on their trips they always used a map.

Smiler spread the map on the floor and he soon found Warminster. A mile and a half south of it was the village of Crockerton in the valley of the River Wylye. Smiler picked out the side road running down to the river bridge at Ford Cottage. He decided to take the map with him. Mrs. Bagnall was not likely to miss it on her weekly visit.

Next, Smiler went up to the bathroom. In ferreting through the bathroom cabinet he had seen two things which he had remembered when he was tussling with his problem.

One was a bottle of tanning lotion and the other was a tube, in a packet, of hair colouring. Dark Brown, the label said. There was a leaflet of instructions with the tube. Smiler read them carefully. One, wet your hair and apply half the cream as you would a shampoo. Two, lather it up and then rinse it off and squeeze surplus water from the hair. Three, apply the rest of the cream and lather well. Now leave the foam on for five, ten or twenty minutes according to how dark you want the hair to go. Four, rinse until the water runs clear. Then set your hair in your favourite style. Smiler grinned. His favourite style!

He stripped off his shirt, ran some water into the basin and set to work. It wasn't as easy as the instructions made it sound. He got the stuff over his face, neck and hands. It was a chocolate brown colour but when he tried to wash it off his hands and face it paled to a sort of sunburnt red. But – after twenty minutes – it looked all right on his hair. He wouldn't have called it dark brown, but it was brown enough – though there was a slight greenness about it. He then took the tanning stuff and worked it into his face and hands and around the back of his neck. It didn't cover the freckles by any means but it looked all right. Quite good, really, Samuel M., he told himself. After that it took him some time to clean up the basin using an old nail brush and a

63

piece of soap from the bath holder. He combed his hair in his natural style, which was straight back without a parting, admired himself, and then began to explore the house for clothes. He was going to keep his own jeans, but he wanted some shirts and socks and something to replace his brown tweed jacket. The clothes he had been wearing at his escape he knew would have been listed in his description by the police.

Major Collingwood was a small man, Smiler soon realized. He found two old blue flannel shirts that would be a fair fit, three pairs of thick woollen socks, a thick grey pullover with a hole in the elbow and a well-worn green anorak with a penknife in one of the pockets. In a cupboard under the stairs he found, too, a pair of Wellington boots that fitted him. As his own shoes were the worse for wear he took them.

Conscious of the liberties he was taking and not overlooking the fact that the moment he went out into civilization he *might* be unlucky and be picked up, Smiler felt he had to try and put himself square with Major Collingwood. He went to the desk in the sitting-room and found a pencil and some sheets of notepaper. It took him some time to get the letter the way he wanted it and he screwed up the spoilt sheets of paper and put them in his pocket.

His letter read:

Dear Major Collingwood, I hope you find this and will understand that I am really only borrowing and will make it alright when my Dad comes back, like paying for the food, and so on, and making up the bottle sixpences if I don't get to do it myself – the sixpences, I mean – when I get the job I hope to get. I have tried not to make a mess, except for some hair dye on the corner of the bathroom curtins. It is a nice house and I hope your wife gets much better.

Signed, Hunted. (P.S. I can't give my right name right now, for reasons)

Also the bike, and some other odds and ends, which maybe I will have returned. Signed, H.

He took the letter to a corner wall cupboard which he had previously looked into. It held bottles of drink and glasses and also a half-empty box of cigars. Smiler reckoned that Mrs. Bagnall was not likely to open the cigar box, but the Major would when he returned . . . perhaps the first evening. He put the letter in the box.

A few minutes later, the cottage locked, Smiler was back in the barn. He stowed all his loose stuff away out of sight under a hay bale. Dressed in a clean shirt and socks, his own jeans, the grey pullover and the anorak and the Wellington boots, he was ready to tackle Warminster.

Shutting the barn door after him, he wheeled the bicycle from the car bay around the back of the barn. A small path led around it and out through a field gate a little above the main gate entrance to the cottage courtyard.

Smiler freewheeled down past the cottage over the grey-stoned river bridge and began to pedal up the slope to the main road. He had already memorized his route from the map which he carried in his anorak pocket along with the handkerchief full of sixpences.

The side road met the main road just above the village of Crockerton – which Smiler later found out was little more than a handful of houses with a post office and general store. He turned right on the main road and twenty minutes later was in Warminster. He had already given himself a lecture on how he was to behave once he had left his shelter. The thing to do was to act naturally and as though you had perfect right to be doing whatever you were doing. People only noticed you if you let your worry about being noticed show. So Smiler rode into Warminster whistling to himself. He parked his bike against a wall in the High Street and went into a newsagent and bought a copy of the local newspaper. It was called *The Warminster Journal and Wilts County Advertiser*, and it cost him fivepence. He was rather pleased with himself that he had already taken out a few sixpences from his handkerchief, so that he didn't have to haul his bundle out in the shop to get at his money. He put the newspaper in his pocket and then cycled around the town a bit to get the lie of the land. Although he was acting naturally, he knew that any moment something could go wrong. That being so, he knew it was wise to have some idea of his bearings and possible escape routes.

He ended up in the free car park near the railway station, rested his bike against a wall and went into the cafeteria. Once inside, the warmth and smell of food made him realize that he was very hungry. He got himself a plate of sausage rolls, two slabs of fruit cake and a cup of coffee and then sat in the window where he could keep an eye on his parked bicycle.

He drank and ate with relish. He decided that it

might be going to turn out his lucky day. He'd got fresh clothes, a fresh appearance, a bike to get about on, and money in his pocket. So far, no one had so much as given him a curious glance, not even a policeman who had walked past him on the pavement as he came out from buying the newspaper.

On the inside of the very first page of the newspaper, under the *Situations Vacant* column – sandwiched between *Experienced Sales Woman wanted to take charge of boutique* (*outer wear and underwear departments*) and (believe it or not and Smiler had to chuckle) *Male Cleaner, full or part-time, required at Warminster Police Station* – was a job going that sounded right up his street. It read:

STRONG LAD wanted, kennel work, experience not necessary, good wages, free lunch. – Mrs. Angela Lakey, Danebury Kennels, Heytesbury.

Well, Samuel M., he thought, that sounded all right, particularly the free lunch. For a moment he remembered longingly Sister Ethel's Irish stews. Whatever else she was not, she was a jolly good cook. Kennels, eh? Well, he liked dogs and he supposed he could be called strong. But where was Heytesbury? He didn't want to be too far from his barn if he could help it. Always supposing he got the job, of course. He took out his map and consulted it. It didn't take him long to find Heytesbury, which was just inside the right-hand edge of the map. It was about three miles south-east of Warminster. He saw that he could take a back road from Heytesbury, through a place called Sutton Veny, and, by another side road, come down to the river below Crockerton without having to go into Warminster at all. He worked out that by this route – if he got the job – he would only have about three or four miles to go.

A few minutes later Smiler was cycling east from Warminster towards Heytesbury along the main road, wondering what Mrs. Angela Lakey would be like.

*   *   *

Yarra, when she left the barn that morning, followed her usual route up the river, keeping just inside the fringe of the woods, but she was unlucky with her hunting. Half a mile from the cottage she put up a drake mallard from the edge of a swampy hollow just inside the wood. The drake went up like a rocket and with him, unexpected by Yarra, went his mate. For a moment the choice of two targets made Yarra hesitate. When she leapt for the female mallard she missed it by a foot. Farther on in the woods she put up a wily old buck hare.

The hare raced away down the wooded slope, twisting and turning. Yarra went after him, but his twists and turns in and out of the trees balked her of a clear, fast run. At the bottom of the slope Yarra expected the hare to turn up or down the river bank. The hare, however, which had lived a long time and knew when something faster than he was on his tail, took off from the bank in a long leap. He splashed into the water and swam across. Yarra pulled up on her haunches and watched him go. Only if she were absolutely forced to it would she take to the water. She watched the hare go caterwise down the river with the strong current and then pull himself out on the other side and disappear. She wrinkled her mask in disgust. She was hungry now and even more restless than she had been on any other day. Because of this she was in a bad temper. She raked the ground with her back legs, her talons sending a shower of dead leaves and twigs and earth flying. An hour later, she was almost at the end of the wooded valley slope where the trees gave way to rough pasture. Fifty yards ahead she saw a lean grey shape at the edge of the water. Yarra froze and watched.

It was a heron standing in two inches of water where the flooded river lapped just over the bank. Below the heron a back eddy had cut a deep pool close in under the bank. It was a favourite fishing place of the heron. When the water was high he knew that the trout and grayling liked to get out of the main current and seek the shelter of the slower pools and back eddies near the bank. Here, too, in winter there was more food than in mid-stream for often the floods washed fat worms, grubs, and insects out of the eroding banks and floated them down for the taking.

Yarra watched the heron for a while and then lowered her body close to the ground and began to stalk him. She kept close to the cover of the winter dry clumps of flags and reeds and the high tufts of dead nettle stems. She had never seen a heron before. The bird moved once, sliding its head an inch lower, dagger-like beak a foot from the stream.

The heron, the wisest and most cautious of birds and possessed of infinite patience, was well aware of Yarra. When she was thirty yards away he had caught, from the corner of his eye, the slight sideways flick of her tufted tail. There were times in Yarra's mounting excitement when she could not stop that momentary flick. But the heron – hungry like Yarra, hungry as all wild birds and beasts are during the lean months of winter – meant to have his meal. He had fished all morning without success. Now, riding in the back eddy, not three feet below him was a good-sized grayling, moving up and down on the alert for food, but so far not rising high enough for the heron to risk a thrust of his beak.

Yarra worked her way forward five yards more and knew that she needed another two yards before she could risk her forward spring and leap. Some instinct in the old heron, who still held Yarra in the corner of his eye as he watched the grayling, told him exactly when he could risk himself no more. Flat to the ground Yarra inched herself forward. She was bunching her muscles for her leap when the grayling below the heron came surfacewards like a slim airship rising. The heron's beak rapiered downwards and took the fish. With the movement Yarra sprang and the heron rose, great grey-pearl wings spreading wide, his long legs tucking up behind him. He planed away and flipped the grayling round in his beak to hold it sideways across the body. Behind him there was a splash. He drifted down river and climbed leisurely into the wind.

Yarra's slashing right forepaw had missed the heron by a foot. Unable to stop her forward progress entirely the front part of her long body came down in the water. For a moment, until her strong haunches could hold and then haul her back, her forepaws and head and shoulders went under.

She pulled herself back on to the bank and shook her head to free her eyes of water. More bad-tempered than ever, she sat on her haunches and licked at her shoulders and neck mantle, grumbling angrily to herself. It was at this moment that she heard down river the sound of men's voices and the bang and rattle of sticks against the trees.

Yarra, disturbed by the noise, headed away up river at a lope. At the edge of the wood she turned uphill, making for the high ground and the wide stretches of pasture, downland and young plantations which she had visited on previous days.

Behind her moved the hunt. It had been well organized by the Cheetah Warden. Making up the hunt were local farmers, gamekeepers and other volunteers. There were also several policemen on foot with walkie-talkie sets to keep in touch with four patrol cars. These cars were set out along the main roads that, with Warminster as its apex, formed a triangle marked at the extremities of its base by Longbridge Deverill (a mile on from Crockerton) to the south and Heytesbury to the south-east. In the middle of the base road joining Longbridge Deverill and Heytesbury was the village of Sutton Veny.

A long line of beaters had been formed early that morning on the southern outskirts of Warminster. Now, spread wide across the valley, the line was moving up river. Beyond Crockerton the line had swept round, formed up along the right bank of the river and was beating its way uphill through a wide stretch of trees and plantations known as Southleigh Woods. At this very moment the Cheetah Warden was standing on the river bank where the hare had

leaped into the river, bending over the spoor ma~~
Yarra had left in a soft patch of mud.

* * *

It was two o'clock in the afternoon when Smi~~
found his way to Danebury Kennels. At the far e~~
of Heytesbury a small road ran off to the left, up~~
narrow valley that sloped down into the main vall~~
of the River Wylye. Danebury House was a mile~~
this road, approached by a short drive. It was~~
large red-bricked house with an untidy lawn~~
front of it and stable and kennel blocks at the re~~
A narrow strip of vegetable garden ran up the h~~
at the back of the house. On the far side of the hou~~
was a thick standing of beech and birch trees.

Smiler rang the front door bell and waite~~
Nothing happened. A cold wind was sweeping~~
the hillside and he was glad of his pullover a~~
anorak. He rang the door bell again. A few minut~~
later he heard a soft shuffling noise inside. The do~~
was opened. Standing before him was a very ta~~
very large woman of about forty. She had a b~~
squarish, red face and an untidy mop of short bla~~
hair. She wore a green sweater tucked into the t~~
of riding breeches. On her feet were long, thic~~
red woollen stockings one of which had a hole in~~
through which part of a big toe showed. She w~~
holding a leg of cold chicken in her hand. As s~~
chewed on a mouthful she surveyed Smiler as thou~~
he were something that the dog had brought hom~~
She finished her chewing and then said brusque~~
"Well, boy?"

Smiler, not sure of his ground, pulled the new~~

paper from his pocket and said, "Please, Ma'am, I've come about the job."

She eyed him for a moment, then looked at the chicken bone, which was now gnawed clean, and tossed it away out to the lawn over his head.

"Oh, you have, have you? Well, let's have a look at you. Turn round." Her voice was brisk, but not unkind, and there was a small twinkle in her dark eyes.

Smiler obediently turned round, facing the lawn. A small Jack Russell terrier came out of the beech coppice, trotted across the grass, picked up the chicken leg and went back into the trees with it. Somewhere at the back of the house what seemed like a pack of a hundred dogs all began to bark and howl together.

From behind him the woman – who was Mrs. Angela Lakey – said briskly, "Right. Nothing wrong with rear view. Turn round."

Obediently Smiler turned about. Mrs. Lakey reached out and took the top of his right arm in a firm grasp and felt his muscles.

"Strong boy wanted," she said. "How strong are you, boy?"

"I'm strong enough, I think, Ma'am."

"Time will show." Mrs. Lakey bent forward a little, peered at his face and said, "You're very sunburnt for this time of the year, aren't you?"

Smiler said quickly, "My skin's always like that, Ma'am."

"Don't call me Ma'am – call me Mrs. Lakey. What I'll call you from time to time – if you get the job – is nobody's business. All right, come in and let's have your particulars." She turned away down

73

the hall. As Smiler followed, she called over her shoulder, "Shut the door. Fresh air's for outside houses, not inside."

She led the way down the hall and into a side room. It was a large, bright room, very lofty, and looked out over the lawn. And it was like no room Smiler had ever seen before. Around the walls were hung fox masks and brushes, glass cases with stuffed fish and birds in them, and a thick patchwork of framed photographs of horses and dogs. Over the big open fireplace, in which burnt a pile of great three-foot length logs, was a large oil painting of a fresh-faced, grey-haired man dressed in white breeches and hunting pink. He sat in a highbacked chair and held a riding crop in one hand and a large, full brandy glass in the other. (Later, Smiler learnt that this was Mrs. Lakey's dead father who had been a Colonel of the Hussars.) Before the fire, between two shabby leather armchairs, was a round table which held a tray of cold food and a full glass with a thick white froth on it which Smiler – because of his father – immediately recognized as a glass of stout. On the back wall of the room were rows of rod-rests with fishing rods stretched across them. Below these was a long low book-case full of volumes packed into it in an untidy jumble. There was a large rolltop desk just inside the door, open, and crammed to bursting with papers and all sorts of odds and ends, including a very old typewriter.

Mrs. Lakey told Smiler to sit by the fire. She went to the desk, rummaged in it, and found a pencil and a piece of very creased paper and came back and sat down opposite him.

She put the paper and pencil on the table, took a

tomato from the tray, bit into it, and said, "Cold snack, today. Milly's away shopping. I've got a lot to do this afternoon so, with your permission, boy –" She gave him a smile which suddenly took all the sternness out of her face. "I'll victual up while I take your particulars. Name?"

In the barn the day before Smiler had gone over in his mind – when he had decided he must go for a job – the answers to all the awkward questions he knew he would be asked, and he had his replies ready.

"Pickering," he said without hesitation. "Johnny Pickering."

Mrs. Lakey wrote it down, and said, "Age?"

"Fifteen and a half."

"Address?"

"I live with my aunt, Mrs. Brown, at Hillside Bungalow, Crockerton. My mother and father . . . Well, they're dead. They was killed in a car accident three years ago."

"Sorry to hear it. Damn cars. They're just murder on the roads. Horse and trap – you got a tumble and a bruising and that was that. Never mind. Times move. Can't alter that. Any previous job? References?"

"No, Ma'am – I mean Mrs. Lakey. I left school Christmas."

"Any experience with animals?"

"No, Mrs. Lakey. But I like 'em. And I had a dog once."

"Willing?" Mrs. Lakey raised the glass of stout to her lips and watched him over the top as she drank.

Puzzled, Smiler said, "I don't really know what

75

you –" Then understanding dawning, he went on quickly, "Oh, yes, I'm willing to take the job. I'd like it."

"No, boy. I mean are you willing to work hard? Sober, industrious, clean and tidy? Always cheerful and no clock watching? Can't have you if you're not all that – and cheerful. Milly hates a gloomy face around the place. Likes boys that whistle and sing and look like the whole day is just one glorious top of the morning to you. And you've got to have a good appetite. Milly can't bear cooking for those who pick and scratch and don't enjoy their victuals. So what do you say?"

A little out of his depth, Smiler said, "I think so, Mrs. Lakey."

"Good." Mrs. Lakey finished her stout. "You seem a likely number to me. Anyway, the advertisement's been in for two weeks and you're the first. Wages – three pounds a week. Free lunch. Sundays off. Half days to be arranged as work permits. Start at seven-thirty. Finish at five this time of the year. Later, as the sun god stays with us longer. Five shillings an hour overtime. Working overalls provided. Anything in that frighten you?"

"No, Mrs. Lakey."

"Well, it would most of the young lay-abouts these days who want a four-hour day, meals off golden plates, two months' paid holiday a year, and then wonder why the country's going to the dogs. Which is the biggest slander on dogs ever uttered. And talking of dogs, let me tell you, my bark is not worse than my bite. My bite is terrible!" She winked at him suddenly.

Smiler, who, it must be confessed, was a bit

confused and uncertain about her, was warmed by the wink. He said, smiling – and Smiler's smile, Sister Ethel had always said, could charm the birds from the trees – "You seem very nice to me, Mrs. Lakey."

Mrs. Lakey looked at him, slowly grinned and then cried heartily, smacking her thigh, "Well now, it's a compliment I'm getting! The first for ten years. Right now, run along with you. Let yourself out. Be here at half-seven tomorrow and we'll see how you shape up."

"Yes, thank you, Mrs. Lakey. I'll do my best."

"You'd better. No less is accepted."

Smiler let himself out and was chased all the way down the drive by the Jack Russell snapping at his back wheel. But Smiler didn't mind.

Going down the valley road to Heytesbury he began to whistle to himself. Everything had gone perfectly. Samuel M., he thought, you carried it off like a hero. You've got a job, as easy as kissing your hand. Milly? Who was Milly, who didn't like gloomy people, only big and cheerful eaters? Well, he'd soon know. And soon know, too, what he had to do. Crikey! – seven-thirty! That meant he would have to be up by six-thirty. Ought he to buy himself an alarm clock in Warminster? Yes, he'd certainly have to do that. If he turned up late, he knew he'd have Mrs. Lakey on his tail, biting worse than her bark. In high spirits he began to swerve from one side of the road to the other. Free lunches and three pounds a week. He was in clover.

*   *   *

In the rough pasture on the plateau at the valley top, Yarra put up a rabbit and killed it within three yards. She carried it into a clump of wind-dwarfed thorn trees and ate it. It was a small, winter-lean rabbit and nowhere near satisfied her hunger.

She moved out of the trees and began to quarter the ground eastwards across the rough amber-coloured grasslands. A hundred yards from the edge of a Forestry Commission plantation of young, waist-high firs she put up a hare. The hare laid its ears back and went like the wind. Yarra raced after it, the memory of the hare she had lost by the river giving her a fierce determination to catch this one. The hare reached the edge of the plantation and found its way blocked by a three-foot high, small-meshed wire fence. It turned right along the fence ten yards ahead of Yarra. She swung across the angle at top speed and leapt for it. Her forepaws smashed down on its back, talons gripping into the fur, and her hindquarters skidded round to crash into the fence. She bit clean through neck and vertebrae, and lay where she had made her kill to eat.

As she began to worry and chew at the soft belly of the hare, a black and white striped Land-Rover came over the ridge of downland away to her right. Yarra heard and saw it simultaneously. She looked up from her meal and watched it. The Land-Rover was moving towards the top end of the fence which ran down the plantation side. Two hundred yards away it turned and began to bump and sway slowly along the fence. Her strong jaws clamped across the belly of the hare, Yarra stopped eating and watched the Land-Rover. For the moment there was no fear in her. The Land-Rover was exactly the same as many she had seen in Longleat Park. She had chased meat trailing on a rope from behind one of them. She had jumped to the cab roof, and even gone to the open cab door of the Cheetah Warden's car when he tossed her a lump of meat which hid worming or other medicines.

She lay watching the Land-Rover come down towards her. As it neared her she let go of the hare, opened her jaws, and gave a slow, warning spit and hiss. She wanted to eat undisturbed.

When the Land-Rover was within forty yards of her, the driver and the man beside him saw her. The driver stopped the car. The man beside him began to speak into his walkie-talkie set. Over the air the news of Yarra's discovery and her location went out to the police cars on the roads and to the policemen who were with the line of beaters now moving slowly up through Southleigh Wood.

The top boundary of the wood lay a few hundred yards down the slope from Yarra. She watched the Land-Rover for a while and, when it did not move, she began to eat. Almost immediately, from behind her, Yarra's quick ears caught the growing sounds of men moving up through the wood. A few of them – who had not yet received the warning of Yarra's discovery – were still beating and rattling their sticks against tree trunks and thickets. The noise disturbed Yarra. She was hungry still and she wanted peace and quiet in which to eat. She stood up, gripped the big hare in her jaws, and leapt over the wire fence into the plantation of young firs. She began to trot fast across the plantation, northwards towards the road that ran from Crockerton, down across the River Wylye and on to Sutton Veny. The noise of men and rattling sticks followed her faintly, so she decided to keep going until she was free of it altogether.

Five minutes later she was across the Crockerton-Sutton Veny road. The noise died away and she padded into a tall clump of wild rhododendrons and couched down to eat her hare. As she did so, from the leaden sky above, the first fat flakes of snow began to drift down, slanting a little in a cold wind that was rising fast.

*　　*　　*

Smiler did not go back to Ford Cottage along the Heytesbury-Sutton Veny road. His anxiety not to be late for work in the morning decided him to return to Warminster and buy a cheap alarm clock in Woolworth's. The girl assistant at the counter was a bit amused when he paid for it all in sixpenny pieces.

"I been saving up," said Smiler.

"Just for an old clock?"

"Present for me mum," he said.

Riding away down the Crockerton road, Smiler thought that it would be nice if it had really been a present for his Mum. He had never known her because she had died a year after his birth. But he knew a lot about her from his father who worshipped her memory.

Before he reached the cottage it began to snow and blow hard. Large, heavy flakes filled the air, whirling and spinning in the wind, and he was glad to pull up the hood of his anorak for protection. Now, as he neared the cottage, he began to think of Yarra. He had to leave the barn door open and, if she came back, he had to do something about her. Yarra, it seemed, was his last problem to tackle before he could start at Danebury Kennels and begin to work his passage for the next nine months.

He hid his bicycle in the orchard at the back of the barn and then slipped round, keeping his eyes open in case Yarra was about already, and opened the barn door. The courtyard had an inch covering of snow. The fast falling flakes rapidly obliterated the footprints he made in crossing to the back door. He shut himself in, leaving the key outside, and then went upstairs to the bathroom to keep vigil on the barn door. He took up with him a packet of biscuits and a pork pie which he had bought in Warminster for his supper. He washed them down with drinks of cold water from the basin tap while he sat on the broad window ledge, one curtain drawn partly back so that he could watch the door.

He kept his fingers crossed that Yarra would not come back. For two reasons he wished this: one, because giving her away when she was on the run like him seemed the act of a traitor, though he knew he had to do it for the safety of other people, especially small children; and two, because it was going to give him a lot of trouble. He didn't want to have to turn out and cycle somewhere to find a telephone because he knew it would mean that he wouldn't be able to come back safely to the cottage until Yarra had been taken. The thought of a night out in the cold made him far from happy. However, Samuel M., he told himself, if she ever comes you have just got to do it.

But Yarra did not come. Smiler watched the barn door until it got dark. There was no sign of Yarra.

Some time after nightfall the snow stopped as suddenly as it had begun and the sky cleared. With the reflection from the snow on the ground and the clear starlit sky, it was quite bright outside. Smiler could easily have seen Yarra if she had come round the barn to gain her shelter. He waited dutifully until the eight-day clock in the hall struck nine (Mrs. Bagnall wound it up once a week when she came). Then he gave up his vigil. He found himself a couple of blankets in one of the spare bedrooms, rolled himself up and went to sleep. He had set the alarm clock for six o'clock in the morning.

6

⤳ *Yarra Moves On* ⤳

The snow saved Yarra from being caught. While she was eating her hare, the beaters came out on to the pasture behind the plantation and met up with the Land-Rover. Messages were sent to the police patrol cars. The hunting line was reformed and swept forward through the young firs as the snow began to thicken.

Yarra was disturbed by the sound of the men crossing the Crockerton-Sutton Veny road fifty yards behind her. She was sighted as she left the cover of her clump of rhododendrons. A couple of the men – unwisely – gave loud shouts that alarmed Yarra even more. She went away at a gallop northwards. She cleared a hedge into a field of young winter wheat, and followed the line of the hedge. The snow falling on her coat melted fast and made her uncomfortable. She hated the wet. As long as she could hear the noises of men behind her she kept going steadily. When the noises died she slackened her pace, but still kept going.

She was in strange country now and her movement was dictated by the lie of the land. She kept close to the hedges and over open ground trotted fast from the cover of bush clump to bush clump. When she met a small wood or coppice she went through it just inside the boundary so that she could break to open ground if danger threatened. Always, when she had the choice, she kept to the high ground rather than the low. Before she crossed any road she waited and watched for the sign of humans before passing over. The snow was so thick now that she could only see about ten yards ahead. The darkness was deepening every minute. The snow and the approach of night were her allies. The snow rapidly filled the tracks she left and made fast going hard work for the men who followed. After an hour they had lost all contact with her. When darkness finally came, with the snow still whirling and beating down, the hunt was called off except for the police patrol cars on the triangulation of roads. If the patrol car men could have known it, they were wasting their time. Yarra had long crossed the side of the triangle which was formed by the Longbridge Deverill-Sutton Veny-Heytesbury road. She had crossed it a few yards short of the point where a road bridge spanned the River Wylye.

Yarra had found the river by hearing the noise of a small waterfall above the bridge. After crossing the road she followed the river downstream. Since missing the heron it was the first time that day that she had seen the river. The river reminded her of her barn shelter. Half a mile down the bank a black shape loomed up out of the darkness and the now thinning snow. It was a dilapidated fishing hut with a large plank seat inside for fishermen to rest on and have their lunch. Drifting snow had melted on the earth floor and formed a shallow puddle of mud and water. Yarra turned into the hut, sniffed around at its smells, and then leapt on to the broad seat. She sat on her haunches, facing the narrow open doorway. She began to groom and clean herself, licking at the inside of her muddy, wet thighs and nibbling at her swelling dugs where the restlessness inside her seemed to be lodged. She had no hunger, but she was tired and bad-tempered. Once, for relief, she uttered an angry, snarling rumble, jaws wide, her face crinkled and her eyes blazing. If anyone had come to the door of the hut at that moment they would not have had a very warm welcome.

Outside the snow stopped and the sky began to clear. Yarra went to bed, on the hard board, twisting and scraping restlessly until she was settled. The river ran by, murmuring quietly to itself. A water vole made a plop as it dropped into the stream and began a night forage down the bankside. A barn owl sailed low on silent wings over the water meadow, quartering the grass and reed tufts for mouse or shrew movement. A fox coming up the river, flicking his pads fastidiously against the thawing snow, caught Yarra's scent from the hut. He decided to have nothing to do with whatever made it, and trotted a wide half circle away from the hut to the river path above it. In an old wren's nest in the roof of the hut a sleepy dormouse burrowed its snout into its fur for warmth and gave a sharp *bleep*. In her light sleep Yarra heard the noise and flicked one stubby ear momentarily. Beyond the river and the railway, cars moved along the Warminster-Heytesbury road, their headlamps washing cottages, hedges and trees with gold light.

The low depression system which had brought the snow up from the west against a strong east wind now moved away east itself. The high pressure area that followed it swung the wind gently into the west and the temperature rose. The snow melted fast and in a couple of hours was gone from all but the sheltered dips and north slopes of the high ground.

At three o'clock in the morning Yarra, stiff and uncomfortable from sleeping on the board seat, woke and left the hut. She went down river and over the railway line. On the southern outskirts of Heytesbury she struck a side road into the village. The night was still, and deserted of all humans. She crossed the river by the road bridge and padded into the village. Her scent roused two dogs in near-by yards to a frenzy of barking. She came out on to the main road at the side of the Angel Inn. She paused for a moment, looked about her, and then crossed the main road and went north up another side road. A few yards up the road on the left-hand side was a large red notice board with a white-painted inscription which read:

IMBER ARMY RANGE
ROAD CLOSED 1 MILE AHEAD

Yarra padded up the tree-bordered road leisurely. The road steepened, mounting the higher contours of a narrow combe running up to the far-stretching plateau of the easterly part of Salisbury Plain. As Yarra passed the drive entrance to Danebury House the Jack Russell terrier saw her. The terrier slept on a rug in the window bay of his mistress's bedroom where the curtains were always drawn back at night. The movement of Yarra on the road caught the alert eye of the unsleeping terrier. He jumped up, body and tail quivering with aggression, and began to bark his head off. From her bed, half in sleep, Mrs. Angela Lakey reached over to the floor – where she kept a small pile of hassock-like cushions for the purpose – and hurled one at the terrier, hitting him amidships as she muttered, "Go to sleep, you old fool!"

Above the house the road cleared the tree line. Where it ran on to the first of the open downland and the wide sweeps of the plain which the Army used for artillery, tank and infantry training, there was a small hut at the side of the road. The road itself was barred with a red-and-white painted drop-post. The hut was not manned at night. Yarra went under the drop-post, and then left the road for the easier going of the rough, wild grassland. She went across country for half a mile, veering away from the road. Ten minutes later, on the side of one of the downland slopes she came across an old, rusted Sherman tank which was used as a target for practice shoots. The turret had been blown askew. The tracks lay collapsed and wrecked on the ground, and there was a large gap in the side of the empty hull. Yarra walked around it, sniffed at the cold metal work, and then looked through into the hull. Somebody had long ago dumped a load of cut bracken inside and covered it with a couple of sacks to make a resting place. To one side of the rough couch were some empty beer bottles and a litter of old cigarette packets and newspapers.

Yarra jumped inside, sniffed around the small interior, and then began to tread the sacks and bracken to make a bed for herself. When she was satisfied she flopped down and stretched out her forelegs, easing her muscles. In a few minutes she was sleeping.

Above her on the inside plates of the tank someone

had written in white chalk – *Bombardier Andy Goran, only 5 yrs and 13 days to serve.* Under that, in another hand, was – *Please leave this hotel as you would wish to find it.*

* * *

The alarm bell brought Smiler out of bed with a jerk. Outside it was still dark. He had a quick wash in the kitchen, ate some of the biscuits he had left, and then tidied everything up in case Mrs. Bagnall made a surprise visit.

When he went out it was to find that the snow had all gone and there was a fresh wind blowing. Seeing the bulk of the barn against the sky, he tiptoed over to it. He didn't want to leave the door open all day, but he wasn't overlooking the fact that Yarra might have come back at some time during the night. He crept down the side of the barn. When he came to the door he reached quickly for the handle and pulled it shut with a slam, dropping the catch. He stood outside listening. If Yarra were in there, the noise would have wakened her and he would hear her movements. No sound came from inside the barn.

A few moments later Smiler was pushing his bicycle up the hill away from Ford Cottage. At the top of the hill he began to ride and soon passed the spot where Yarra had crossed the road with her hare. But Smiler was not thinking about Yarra. He was giving himself a talking-to for not having thought of buying a bicycle lamp in Warminster. Although it was light enough for him to ride without danger, it was still officially dark enough for him to be showing a light. The last thing he wanted was to be stopped by some patrolling local policeman and have to answer awkward questions.

Warm and snug in his pullover and anorak, he turned left at the crossroads in Sutton Veny. He had a good memory for maps, a "bump of locality" as Sister Ethel's Albert used to say. Thinking of Sister Ethel and her Albert, Smiler decided that some time soon he would have to get a message to them that he was all right. He didn't want them going about thinking that maybe he was dead, or anything like that, and then writing off to his Dad and putting the wind up him. The problem of how he could send a message, without giving himself away, occupied him as he rode.

Some time later, the light in the easterly sky brightening fast now, he passed over the Wylye river bridge at the point where Yarra had crossed the road on her way downstream. To his left he could hear the sound of the little waterfall. From the river bridge it was not far to the main road that led to Heytesbury.

Smiler arrived at Danebury House at twenty minutes past seven. He was met at the drive gate by the Jack Russell whose name, he later learned, was Tonks when he was not in disgrace, and Mister Tonks when he was, which was pretty often. Tonks gave him a yapping welcome and then trotted up the drive alongside him.

Smiler was met at the back door by Mrs. Angela Lakey. She was dressed as he had seen her the day before, except that she now wore gum boots and a red beret.

She greeted him heartily, smacking him on the back, and said, "Morning, Boy. Punctual. That's

what I like to see. Begin as you mean to go on."
The whole time he was to be at Danebury House
she never called him anything else but "Boy".

She gave him a cup of hot coffee in the kitchen,
and instructed him in his duties. She then took him
outside and "showed him the ropes" as she called it.

At Danebury House, Mrs. Lakey – and her
sister, Miss Milly Finn – ran breeding kennels for
English and Gordon setters. They also had boarding
kennels where people going on holiday, or Army folk
going off on a tour of duty abroad, could leave their
dogs. There was a small section, too, which held
room for about eight cats. Mrs. Lakey would have
nothing to do with these. She didn't rate cats very
high in the animal creation. But Miss Milly did and
they were her responsibility, though Smiler had to
look after them most of the time. Miss Milly ran
the house, did the cooking, and kept the books
without any outside help.

In addition to these animals, there were also two
hunters in a stable near the beech copse. These
Mrs. Lakey hired out to people who wanted to ride
or hunt – but she took very good care that they were
the kind of people who understood and could handle
horses. There was a chestnut mare, Penny, and a
bay gelding called – for some reason Smiler never
discovered – Bacon. Bacon, he soon found, liked to
give you a quick nip if you didn't watch him. Penny
was very even-tempered except that now and then
she would see things under her nose that no one else
could see – invisible fairies or dwarfs or snakes. Then,
she would leap sideways or pirouette like a ballet
dancer on her hind legs – and off you would come
unless you were wise to her weakness. Over the

stable loft there was a pigeon cote full of white fantail doves. In a run at the bottom of the vegetable garden lived twelve white Leghorn hens – known as the Apostles. At the back of the kennel runs was a storehouse where all the hound meal and dog-and-cat meat was kept and cooked in a big boiler.

Although Smiler had nothing to do with the horses to begin with, he had plenty on his hands. It was, he soon learned, his job to cut up and cook the dog meat, weigh up the hound meal, feed all the dogs and cats and keep their water bowls full. He had to clean out the kennels twice a week and lay new bedding, feed and water the hens and collect the eggs, and exercise the setters in the five-acre paddock beyond the beech copse. He had to groom and brush all dogs twice a week, fetch in the logs for the house from the wood stack, wash down the horse-box, and dig the vegetable garden when he had any spare time. Also it was his duty to keep an eye on Tonks who was at perpetual war with the fantails and the Twelve Apostles.

On the first morning, as Mrs. Lakey rattled off all this to him and "showed him the ropes", his head spun and he felt that he would never be able to manage. After a few days, however, he was managing easily, though – since he hated digging – he made sure that he didn't often have spare time for that. His free "working overalls" turned out to be ex-Army stock, green, and covered all over with brown, yellow and black camouflage markings.

Overwhelmed a bit by all this on the first day, the most cheering thing for Smiler was Miss Milly, who was younger than Mrs. Lakey. She was short and plump, fair-haired and fresh-faced, and jolly and kind. Her kitchen was spotless and smelled always of baking and cooking. She never called him "Boy". Right from the first it was "Johnny" which was a bit awkward, now and then, when she called him because he forgot that he was Johnny and didn't answer.

Smiler's first free lunch was a revelation that banished from his mind any culinary prowess that his Sister Ethel could show.

When he was called for lunch, Miss Milly said, "Gum boots outside the door, overalls off, face and hands washed, and then to table, Johnny." She talked a bit like Mrs. Lakey but there was always laughter and kindness in her voice.

Johnny ate in the kitchen by himself. After he was served lunch, the two sisters would have theirs together in the dining-room. That first day he was served steak-and-kidney pie, Brussels sprouts, and butter-creamed mashed potatoes. He had a glass of milk to drink with it and fresh-baked bread. For "afters" he had a great slab of treacle tart with custard and could have finished up with Cheddar cheese and home-made bread if he had had room for it. Later, when he really got into his working stride, he never missed the cheese and bread.

That first day there was only one personally awkward moment for Smiler.

At the end of the day he came into the scullery next to the kitchen where he had been instructed to hang his working overalls each night. Miss Milly was there, polishing a pair of tall, black riding boots belonging to Mrs. Lakey.

"How long does it take you to get home, Johnny?" asked Miss Milly.

"Oh, not long, Miss Milly." He had been instructed to call her that.

Miss Milly nodded and then stared thoughtfully at the sheen she had worked on one of the boots and said, "I know Crockerton well. Hillside Bungalow? Can't recall that, Johnny. Where is it?"

Smiler hadn't the faintest idea where it was because he had just made up the name without giving it a location. But he gathered his wits and said, "Well . . . it's sort of . . . Well, you know, not in the village and not exactly outside of it."

Miss Milly grinned. "That's a good description for finding a place on a dark night. New, is it? One of the new bungalows?"

Smiler wasn't going to be pinned down, so he said, "Well . . . it's not really new. Nor old either. It's sort of past the post office and then down a little sidepath towards the river."

"Near the old millhouse, you mean?"

"That's right, Miss Milly."

"Well, ride home carefully."

From Mrs. Lakey he got a different farewell for the day. As he wheeled his bicycle out of the yard, Mrs. Lakey came round the corner on Penny which she had been exercising in the paddock. She pulled up, looked at her wrist-watch, and said, "Finished for the day, Boy?"

"Yes, Ma'am . . . I mean, Mrs. Lakey."

"Shut the hens up?"

"Yes, Mrs. Lakey."

"Good. Well, Boy, we'll make something of you. You move well. Should stay the course if your wind holds. Right, cut along, Boy. Get a good night's rest and come back fighting fit in the morning."

She moved off on Penny and Smiler rode down the drive, accompanied by Tonks as far as the gate.

In Heytesbury he stopped at a garage and bought himself a bicycle lamp with the last of his hoard of sixpenny pieces. The garage assistant looked at the money, looked at Smiler, winked and said, "Been robbing the poor box, then?"

*   *   *

Yarra left her tank shelter not long after first light. Outside she stretched herself and then spent some minutes giving herself a good grooming. It was a clear, almost cloudless day with a brisk wind blowing across the plain from the south-west. A solitary lark, emboldened by the bright sun, climbed aloft and held a short song practice for the promised coming of Spring.

Her grooming finished, Yarra loped away down hill from the tank. At the bottom of the dip she found a pool of rain water and drank. For the next two hours she circled wide over the plain and saw many other old tank targets dotted along the down sides and hill crests. She was on the eastern portion of Salisbury Plain, an area about six miles long and five miles deep. The whole plain was about twenty to thirty miles long, a vast expanse of rolling, dun-coloured grass and downland, broken here and there by smooth, shallow valleys and combes and an occasional isolated clump of trees on a ridge. In some of the deeper valleys were scrub and thorn areas. Over the whole stretch there was not a plough-patch to be seen, not a domestic animal to be found grazing. The land all belonged to the

Ministry of Defence and the public for the most part was excluded. When people were admitted on special days or at the week-ends they had to keep to the rough tracks and roads which criss-crossed the plain and which were marked at frequent intervals with notices that read:

DANGER – UNEXPLODED MISSILES
DO NOT LEAVE THE CARRIAGEWAYS
YOU HAVE BEEN WARNED

When the red flags were flying at the Army entrance points to the plain, known as Vedettes, nobody was allowed entry except the military personnel engaged in training or manoeuvres. For the whole of the great expanse of the plain there were five Land Wardens who patrolled the roads and tracks in Land-Rovers to see that no unauthorized persons came into the area. For the eastern portion of the plain, where Yarra was, there were two Land Wardens.

Great tank tracks scored the slopes and plateaux of the plain. Where the tanks had permanent road crossings these were marked with black-and-yellow-topped posts to warn car drivers of the thick mud they might expect to find on the road.

It was a wide, desolate area given over by day to the troops, though even they were lost in its vastness. Also, it was the home of many wild creatures – the hare, the fox, the stoat and weasel, the wild deer, the rat and the rabbit and a few families of feral cats – household pets that had wandered into the wilderness and reverted to their ancestors' old way of life. Sometimes a sheep-killing rogue dog found sanctuary on the barren terrain and made forays at night down into the farmlands that bordered it. In the air above the plain flew the buzzard, the kestrel and the sparrow hawk, all of them ever alert for the movement below of pheasant, partridge, and the small birds that lived in the tall grasses, the thickets and patches of wood. In fact, although the plain looked barren, it teemed with life – raven, rook, and wood pigeon, all the mice and shrews, and the gentle slow-worm, the inoffensive grass snake, and the swift adder. At one time, unhappily extinct now and commemorated by the name of an inn on the western part of the plain, one could have seen the great bustard.

This then was the area into which Yarra had moved and close to which Smiler had found a job. Just as Smiler on his first day of work had eaten well, so did Yarra as she roamed the plain.

Walking away from the rainwater pool, she saw the movement of a field mouse in the grass and caught it in a single bound. Like an ordinary cat, she played with it for a while, throwing it around her, bounding and leaping about it as though it were still alive and trying to escape her. Then she carried it in her mouth for a little while, became bored with it, and dropped it for a scavenging crow to find an hour later.

She put up a rabbit from behind a boulder and raced, doubled and twisted with it at her leisure and finally killed and ate it. Half an hour later she flushed one of the feral cats from a clump of gorse. It was a three-year-old tabby tom. He streaked to a nearby solitary dead pine and found sanctuary on a branch eight feet above Yarra. He arched his back, lofted his tail stiffly, and spat and swore down at her. Yarra sat back on her haunches, eyed him, and spat and hissed back. But she had no desire to leap or climb after him. Maybe, deep within her, was some feeling that made her content with a brief passage of family formalities.

At mid-day, she lay in the sun just below a ridge top, her orange and black pelt merging into her background so that from fifty yards she was practically invisible. A mile away, on a distant slope, sat an old Churchill tank. As Yarra blinked her golden-amber eyes against the sun, watching the tank, there was a loud crack of noise away to her right. Almost immediately, alongside the tank, the earth fountained upwards in a plume of mud, grass tufts and black smoke. Yarra flinched at the sight, and gave a silent gape of her jaws to show her displeasure.

There was another crumping, cracking noise from the left. This time an anti-tank shell hit the Churchill in the fore part of its hull. A large piece of plating flew up into the air, spinning like an ungainly black butterfly, the whirr of its clumsy wings coming distinctly across the valley to Yarra's keen ears.

Yarra got up and moved away, going over the downland ridge behind her and seeking another resting place. She was at the start of learning many lessons. She was to come to know the sound of guns firing, the crack of a rifle, the mad chatter of automatic weapons, the whip-crack of artillery and the slow, heavy thump of large calibre shells exploding – and to move away from all such sounds. She was to come to recognise the deployed line of battle-dressed infantrymen moving up to a crest, the rattle of an

approaching tank or troop carrier, the movement of
Army jeeps on road and grassland, the monstrous
gnat-song of helicopters in the air above – and to
move away from them all. But on most days the
plain was free to her and the other animals and birds
during the early morning hours and again in the
slow-stretching evening hours, from five or six
o'clock onwards, when the Army packed up its
warlike gear and went back to barracks and billets
at the sprawling garrisons and encampments of
Larkhill, Bulford, Tidworth and Warminster. All
this Yarra was to learn, but not without danger and
many a sharp lesson, given once and not forgotten.

On this, her first day, she moved and hunted in
comparative peace. She killed two hares in the
afternoon and ate them both. Since she only needed
about three pounds of meat a day to keep her
satisfied, and had now had far more than this, she
hunted no more. It was this that saved the life of a
young deer that, hidden in a stretch of bracken,
scented her as she approached downwind. The deer
broke cover and went away in a long, leaping,
bounding run. Momentarily Yarra moved in pursuit,
impelled by a natural reflex action. But after a few
yards, she broke off the chase and stalked into the
bracken from which the hind had broken. She found
the deer's couching place, sniffed around it and then
lay down and rolled and scrubbed her back on
it, taking pleasure from the deer's scent just as a
dog rolls in ecstasy over the long dead body of
rabbit or rat.

As the light began to go from the sky, and great
banks of high-towering, dark rain-clouds slowly
formed in the west and began a ponderous sweep

across the plain, Yarra went back to her tank. She found her way easily for at no time during the day had she been more than a couple of miles from it. She slipped into the hull as darkness came and sniffed around. She played for a moment with an empty beer bottle and then stopped because she disliked the noise it made on the steel flooring. She arranged her bed, dropped to it, stretched herself, shook her head and settled to sleep.

*　　*　　*

Seven or eight miles away Smiler was settling down for the night in the barn. He had arrived home at last light. The door had been shut all day so that he knew Yarra could not be in the barn. In fact, the garage assistant (all the local inhabitants were full of gossip about the escaped cheetah) from whom he had bought his bicycle lamp had told him that the radio had reported that it was thought that the cheetah had gone down river towards Wilton and Salisbury. Anyway, she hadn't been sighted by anyone that day.

With Ford Cottage itself all neat and tidy, and no obvious signs in it of Smiler's brief occupation, Smiler now took up permanent quarters in the barn. He had everything there he needed. He had his clothes, the borrowed radio, two borrowed blankets from the spare bedroom, a small store of food he had bought in a Sutton Veny grocer's on the way back, and drinking and washing water in a bucket he had found in the lower part of the barn. He had his bicycle lamp for light should he need it, soft hay to sleep on, the alarm clock to wake him in the morning, and the bolt across the trapdoor so that no one could take him by surprise during the night. The first day of a new regime was almost over. He had got himself fixed up. He had got himself a job that paid well and gave him one square meal a day. Samuel M., he told himself, you are in clover. He switched on the radio very low and lay back for some pleasant listening before he drifted off to sleep.

Back at Danebury House in the large, untidy sitting-room Mrs. Angela Lakey was sitting in one of the leather armchairs before the fire, smoking a cigar and sipping now and then at a glass of whisky. Tonks was asleep before the fire. Miss Milly was sitting in the other chair, writing out the monthly bills for the kennel boarders. She sipped now and then at a glass of sweet marsala wine of which she was very fond, although it tended to give her indigestion.

Mrs. Lakey said, "Well, what do you think of the boy, Milly?"

"He's a good boy, Jelly." Jelly was her nickname for her sister and Mrs. Lakey had learned to put up with it over the years, though she didn't like it.

"Could be," announced Mrs. Lakey slowly. "Tonks has taken to him. That's a good sign."

"I've taken to him, too," said Miss Milly, and added, "The next time I'm over Crockerton way I think I'll call in and have a word with his aunt." Then, after sipping at her glass of marsala again, she went on, "And Jelly – you were doing your mean act with him. For all the work that Johnny has to do three pounds a week is not enough. He should have four."

"Nonsense, Milly. Three's ample. Boys should

work for the love of a job. All they want is a little pocket money to keep them happy."

"Four," said Miss Milly. "He's got to pay his way with his aunt."

"Three, Milly."

"Four, Jelly."

Mrs. Lakey sighed and said, "Toss you for it."

"Right," said Miss Milly and she produced a well-worn double-headed shilling from her handbag. She spun it on the table and, as it revolved on the polished surface, said, "Heads four, tails three."

The coin settled down and showed a head.

"I win," said Miss Milly, smiling.

Grinning, Mrs. Lakey said, "You always do."

"Only when right is on my side. Anyway, I'm glad for Johnny. He's got a nice smile."

"And you've got a soft heart, Milly."

"And so have you, Jelly. Only you don't show it often. Yes, as soon as I get a chance I'll go and see his aunt. Poor Johnny, how awful losing his mother and father like that."

7

∽ The Lost Village ∽

When Smiler arrived at work the next morning he was greeted first by Tonks, and then by Mrs. Lakey at the back door and invited in for a cup of coffee. This, he discovered, was to be the usual custom. Over the coffee Mrs. Lakey told him he was such a likely-looking lad and showed such signs of being a good worker that she had decided to up his wages to four pounds a week. However, he would have to take on cleaning out the stables and feeding Penny and Bacon. Later, if he showed any signs of taking to it, she would teach him how to ride. "Though," she said, "you're going to be too big, Boy, ever to make a jockey. But you look as though you may have a good seat and a fair pair of hands."

During the following days Smiler buckled down to his job with cheerfulness and a good will, and soon knew his way around the place. Among the animals some soon became great favourites with him.

Of the setters he particularly liked two. One was a yellow and white English setter dog called – though not on his Kennel Club pedigree – Lemon Drop. The other was a black and tan Gordon setter bitch. Although called Fairy, she was just the opposite, being big, heavy and clumsy, but with a fair turn of speed whenever she put up a rabbit. When he took the dogs for the afternoon walk around the paddock and up the little valley beyond it, he always had to keep an eye on Lemon Drop because the dog had a habit of wandering. Wherever Smiler went Tonks would go with him – unless he was away with Mrs. Lakey somewhere.

There was plenty of coming and going at Danebury House. People came to look over puppies they were thinking of buying, people brought and fetched cats and dogs from the boarding kennels, and once the Hunt met there before going off one Saturday. It was on that day that Smiler saw Mrs. Lakey in all her glory. She was mounted on Bacon, wearing a black top hat, a creamy white cravat at her throat, black hunting boots on which Miss Milly had put a shine that, she said, "would wipe the eye of the sun itself."

Smiler got to know all the calling tradesmen: the butcher, the baker, the milkman and the dogs' meat man who called twice a week. And everyone got to know Smiler (Johnny) and to accept him. Miss Milly fussed over him like a mother hen and he fed like royalty. Outside, Mrs. Lakey kept him hard at work. He grew stronger and harder, and could hump a hundred-weight sack without trouble, and wheel twelve loads of stable and kennel litter in an hour without being troubled for breath. After two weeks Mrs. Lakey put him up on Penny and gave him his first riding lesson. It ended with him being thrown into a quaggy, watercress pool in the middle of the paddock when Penny saw one of her private fairies. But at the end of the first week Mrs. Lakey said, "Good, Boy. You look less like a sack of hay on a seesaw than you did."

On the road between Crockerton and Heytesbury people got to know Smiler on his morning and evening passage and waved to him. At Ford Cottage he had fallen into an easy routine. He slept in the barn and before he left hid all his belongings away under the hay. He went into the cottage every night when he got back and checked the mail which had been delivered in case there was a postcard from Major Collingwood to Mrs. Bagnall saying that he was coming back. He saw Mrs. Bagnall once or twice as he passed Lodge Cottage on the Sutton Veny road. On Sunday – which was usually his day off unless Miss Milly or Mrs. Lakey wanted him to do something special for overtime work – he would get on his bike and explore the country and then go into Warminster to the cinema in the evening. He earned four pounds a week and saved the best part of it, slowly amassing a small hoard of pound notes which he kept in a tin box behind a loose board in the barn loft.

Before the first month was out he found a way to write to his brother-in-law, Albert, and his sister, Ethel. One day the dogs' meat man (who had taken a liking to Smiler) said he was going down to Southampton on a Saturday to see a football match. He asked Smiler if he would like to come along. So, Smiler took a Saturday off and worked the Sunday and went with him. In Southampton he posted a letter to Albert and Ethel. It read:

Dear Sis and Albert, Don't worry about me I am doing fine and am shipping to sea for six months. Cant tell you the name natcheraly. Not to worry I am in the pink.

Samuel M.

Albert – against his will, but forced by Ethel –

took the letter to the Bristol police. They passed the information on to the Southampton police, and the Southampton police made a few enquiries around the docks and shipping companies but "natcheraly" got nowhere!

So there was Smiler, nicely settled between Danebury House and Ford Cottage. The weeks went by. February, which was a real fill-the-dyke month that year, passed. March came with its high winds and occasional days which were hot enough to make one think of summer. The hazel and willow catkins bloomed and the snowdrops gave way to daffodils and crocuses. The drab, flat winter grasses began to show a faint new green. In the gardens there was early almond and cherry blossom. Once or twice smart snowstorms returned to remind everyone that winter wasn't going to pass without a few last skirmishes.

Every fortnight Smiler went into Warminster and bought himself a tube of dye and some tanning lotion from Woolworth's to give his hair and face a new dressing. Every time he did so Mrs. Lakey would look at him the next morning oddly. Miss Milly would smile over the kitchen table at lunch-time and think how brown and healthy Johnny was from all the outdoor work.

Once when Smiler was in Woolworth's buying his dye and sun-tan, he also went on to the electrical counter to get a battery for the transistor set from the cottage which he still used at night.

As he was looking over the display, a voice said, "Hullo, you."

Smiler looked up to find himself meeting the dark eyes of Ivy (who liked to be called Pat) Bagnall.

"Hullo," said Smiler.

"You're Johnny Pickering, aren't you? Remember me?"

Smiler said, "Course I do. Pat Bagnall."

"How you been then?" asked Pat.

"Not bad."

"You still living in Warminster?"

"Yes, sort of. Just outside."

"Ever go to the Youth Club?"

"No. I don't go for that scene."

"You ought to try it. Like to come one night with me?" She said it with a smile and a little toss of her head which Smiler liked. At the same time he knew that the last place he wanted to visit was a Youth Club. People who ran Youth Clubs asked questions and took an interest in you.

"Can't really," he said. "I work most nights."

"Where?"

Smiler did some quick thinking and replied, "Oh, a garage down Heytesbury way. On the pumps."

"Every night?"

"Well, most." To change the subject, he went on quickly, "You like it here?"

"So-so. But I'm thinking of getting another job."

Smiler, not wishing to be further involved, and giving up the idea of buying a battery from her, said, "Well, see you around some time."

He moved down the crowded length of the shop. The girl at the cosmetics counter had seen him talking to Pat. After work she said to Pat, "Who's that chap I saw you talking to? One with a green anorak."

"Oh, him. He's just a chap I know."

"Dyes his hair, don't he? And uses suntan stuff?"

"Course not."

"Does you know. Comes in regular once a fortnight." The girl giggled. "And they say us girls is the vain ones."

That night, as Mrs. Lakey and Miss Milly sipped at their after dinner whisky and marsala, Mrs. Lakey said out of the blue, "That Boy."

"What boy?" asked Miss Milly.

"Johnny."

"What about him?"

"He's good with animals. Got Captain Black's brute of an Alsatian right under his thumb. Dog would lick his boots if he said so."

"Animals are good judges," said Miss Milly.

"So would people be if they used their ears and eyes. Anything about him ever worry you, Milly?"

"No, Jelly. He does his work and he's got a good appetite. Polite, cheerful, and clean – for a lad. Why?"

"I just wondered, Milly. Just wondered. Did you ever get to see his aunt?"

"Not yet. I haven't been over that way."

"Well, don't bother about it. I met old Judge Renton in Warminster yesterday. He lives Crockerton way. Asked him about the boy and his aunt. Said she was a good, solid body. Spoke well of the boy, too. So don't bother, Milly. You've got enough on your hands already without going parish visiting."

Mrs. Lakey picked up a newspaper and hid behind it.

* * *

While Smiler was settling in at Danebury House, Yarra was settling on the plain. By the beginning of April she was very close to her cubbing time and had grown heavy and full in the belly. She could still lope and trot tirelessly. But now, when she hunted a hare or rabbit, she killed her quarry quickly because she did not like to keep at top speed for long.

She found food easy to come by and knew a dozen places where she could always get water to drink. She lived mostly in the tank she had first picked for her sleeping quarters, but if she roamed far she had five other sleeping places, two of them nature-made lairs and three in abandoned tanks and lorries.

At Longleat Park there had been no news of her since they had lost her in the snowstorm. This worried the Cheetah Warden because he felt that she might have had some accident and been killed. She could easily have fallen down an old well or been shot by some farmer or keeper by mistake and then buried to avoid awkwardness over her death. Or she could have been swept away in a river flood. Or she could have caught some disease which had killed her. Her carcase might be quietly rotting in some lonely spinney or gully. But in his own mind the Cheetah Warden did not really believe any of these possibilities. On the other hand he could not understand why she had not been sighted. He had not overlooked the possibility that she might have found her way up on to the plain. As the Army authorities would not give permission for a full-scale drive across it unless there was a definite sighting, the Cheetah Warden had asked the Land

Wardens who ranged the plain to keep an eye out for Yarra.

So far none of them had sighted her, but two of them had passed quite close to her in the course of the passing weeks. They missed seeing her when she was in the open at a distance because her coating merged into the background in perfect camouflage. Chiefly, however, they missed her because she moved about during the early morning and late evening. During the day, if she heard the sound of a car or tank engine, the crackle of firing or the shouting of the soldiers, she went into hiding at once. The nearer her time came, the more cautious she grew.

But this did not mean that Yarra had not been seen. Many of the birds and animals knew her. A carrion crow marked her morning and evening rounds. When she killed he would wait, circling aloft until she had eaten, and then move down for his pickings. The deer knew her and her scent and moved fast the moment it came on the wind to them. One or two lucky hares, who had escaped her, knew her.

The only human who saw Yarra during this period was Smiler. It was on an April day when the fat leaf buds were shedding their wrappings and beginning to green the trees, when the sheltered banks held the pale full glow of primroses, and some of the early blackbirds and thrushes had begun to lay. Smiler lost Lemon Drop on a walk up the coppice-studded valley. He only kept on leads the boarding dogs who were allowed out. Lemon Drop and Fairy and the resident setters were allowed free. Mostly they were obedient to him and came when he called. But Lemon Drop was a wanderer. When Smiler got back to the kennels he missed him. It was four o'clock and both Miss Milly and Mrs. Lakey were out. He knew he would be in trouble if they came back and he had to report Lemon Drop missing. He put the other dogs in their kennels and went away in search of him. He knew exactly where he would most likely be. Right at the top of the valley there was a small wood of lofty, smooth-barked beech trees. Lemon Drop had a passion for squirrel hunting there, and the squirrels now were out and about from their semi-hibernation.

Smiler went up the valley path at a steady trot towards the beeches. When he was fifty yards from the trees he heard Lemon Drop barking. He called and went in after him. From the sound of the barking he could tell that he was at the top end of the wood which was bounded with a wire-netting fence to prevent cattle straying through to the plain.

He found Lemon Drop at the foot of a tall beech tree. The tree grew right alongside the fence and some of its branches hung over it. Lemon Drop was looking upwards and barking furiously. He took no notice of Smiler as he approached. He ran round the tree, whining and barking, and then raised himself against the smooth bark of the great bole, looking upwards.

Smiler looked upwards, too, and immediately stood transfixed. Lying along a thick branch that ran outwards from the tree was Yarra. She was looking down at the dog from a height of about fourteen feet. Although Yarra was not unduly disturbed, she now and again gave a threatening hiss and spit and switched her long tail to and fro irritably. The perch on the branch was a favourite resting place of hers when she found herself in this part of the plain. She liked to lie up there, catching the warmth of the westering sun.

For a few moments Smiler saw her clearly, the sunlight catching her orange-and-black-spotted pelt, one foreleg dangling over the bough. Then she scented him, turned her head, and saw him. He was a big human being and she knew better than to stay where she was. She rose and moved quickly outwards along the branch. She jumped from it in a great leap that took her clear over the boundary fence, and went across the grass in a long, fast gallop.

Lemon Drop rushed to the fence, barking and growling. Smiler went after the dog and caught him. He slipped the lead on to his collar and held him. Away in the distance Yarra was soon lost over a rise in the ground.

Smiler walked away, dragging Lemon Drop after him, protesting and whining for a while. Smiler knew all about the plain now and how it was used by the Army. It was a wild place and, he argued with himself, soldiers could well look after themselves. So, why shouldn't Yarra be left to her freedom there? In a way he was glad to have seen her. Locally there were all sorts of rumours about her. That she had been killed, that she'd been seen well south of Salisbury in the New Forest, and that she'd gone back to Longleat and was hanging around in the woods there. Joe Ringer – the dogs' meat man who had become very friendly with Smiler – said that he knew for certain she'd been shot by a farmer, skinned, and her pelt turned into a rug for the front parlour. But Joe always had a different story from anyone else. In fact Joe was full of stories and most of them came from his own imagination.

Smiler decided that the best thing he could do was to forget that he had ever seen Yarra and to keep the dogs away from the plain. If he reported Yarra to Mrs. Lakey it would only bring the police and other people around and he would have to tell his story and attract too much attention to himself. Reporters would want to know who he was and where he lived, and might even want to ask questions of his non-existent aunt at Hillside Bungalow! That would put the fat in the fire. No, Samuel M., he told himself – just pretend you never saw her.

When Smiler got back to Danebury House Mrs. Lakey and Miss Milly still had not returned, but Joe Ringer was there. His little green van was in the yard and he was off-loading the dogs' meat into the store house.

"Where've you been then, Johnny? All the dogs back and you not here. I could have pinched the silver from the house and helped myself to a dozen eggs."

"Lemon Drop went on the loose," said Smiler. "Had to go and get him."

"Itchy feet and a sharp nose he's got. But too big for delicate work like . . . well, let's leave it at that." Joe winked.

Smiler knew exactly what he meant, because everyone knew that Joe was a poacher in his spare time. Joe was a small, wiry middle-aged man, with very dark hair and a dark complexion. He had gypsy blood in him. He had worked around Warminster and Heytesbury for fifteen years earning a living trading, knackering and poaching. He lived in a small cottage in a side lane running off the Heytesbury-Warminster road.

The cottage was close to the river. There was an untidy sprawl of tin sheds and huts behind it which were filled with all sorts of junk. Joe lived alone and did for himself. And he lived like a king. One way and another, whether in season or out, Joe fed himself and his friends on the fat of the land – trout, pheasant, partridge, jugged hare, delicious rabbit stews, baked grayling and – come Christmas time – turkey, duck, and stuffed pork. Eating was Joe's joy – though he never put on weight. Also, there was always a large cask of cider just inside his kitchen door. When Joe had taken Smiler to the Southampton football match, he had given Smiler supper afterwards. Smiler had been so full of food and cider going home that he could hardly cycle straight. Smiler liked Joe, and Joe liked Smiler. Sometimes Joe let Smiler drive the old green van up and down the road between Danebury House and Heytesbury.

And Joe knew perfectly well that Smiler (Johnny to him) didn't have an aunt living at Crockerton. Joe, who was curious about everyone and everything, had made a few careful enquiries. Joe was always on the look-out for bits of useful information that he could turn into an honest shilling or two. But Joe had a mystery in his own life, too. He guessed that Smiler had also. And because Joe liked Smiler – he kept what he knew to himself and asked no questions.

Joe now said, "What you doing Sunday next?"

"Nothing," said Smiler.

"Well then, I got an order for some early peewees' eggs. Like to help me collect 'em?"

"Peewees?"

"Peewits, Johnny. Lapwings. Them birds what nest up on the downs. Could be some laying already. Ten bob a dozen I can get. Give you a quarter of what we make? All right?"

"Yes. I'd like that, Mr. Ringer."

"Right then. My place. Eight o'clock. And don't blab it around. The eggs is protected."

"Protected?"

"By law. Shouldn't take 'em. But if nobody did the things they shouldn't the world would stop going round. While we're out I'll show you somethin' too. Place where my old Daddy used to live."

*　　*　　*

While Joe was talking to Smiler, Yarra was making her way northwards across the plain to her sleeping place. The evenings were much longer now. After the soldiers had gone there was still a good two hours of daylight. It was a time when Yarra liked to be abroad and hunting.

Because of the cubs she carried there were days when she was full of hunger and would eat three hares and any odd partridges or birds she could flush up. There were other days when the hunger forsook her altogether, and she just liked to roam to ease her restlessness. This was one of those days.

Above her in the evening sky as she moved the lapwings – whose eggs Joe was going after – were flying. Now and again when Yarra, unsuspecting, passed close to a nest a bird would come tumbling and diving down at her with a fierce, rushing sound of wings. Yarra ignored them.

Yarra went north for about three miles, then dropped to a shallow valley which had a road running through it. She crossed a small brook bordered with watercress patches. As she jumped it a snipe went up from a clump of marsh grass by the water and zig-zagged away down the valley in a swift, clipping flight.

Yarra crossed the road and went up a long barren slope, studded here and there with turf-topped weapon pits. She went right to the top of the long slope and came out on its ridge.

Below her was a long, narrow combe running away to her right towards the far stretches of the plain. From where she stood the hillside dropped very sharply to the valley bottom. For a quarter of a mile either side of her the hillside was too steep for the passage of tanks or troop carriers so that its peace was never disturbed. Tank tracks ran up the bed of the valley. On the far side, and lower down, there was a group of tall trees. Beyond them showed a narrow piece of road and a collection of village houses, roofs and windows shattered, gardens wild and overgrown, and not a soul to be seen moving. Beyond the houses on a rising slope, partly seen through bushes and trees, was a grey-stoned church. Its tower reached up to the sky and was ornamented with five tall stone pinnacles.

During the day, as Yarra knew, the village was often busy with soldiers and their vehicles. But at night it was always deserted. It was a village lost and isolated in the miles and miles of the plain, and it was a village which held no human life except when the soldiers came.

Yarra dropped down the valley side. Fifteen feet below the ridge grew four or five mixed ash and alder trees, their bases screened with blackberry and thorn growths. Behind them was a chalky patch of loose ground outside an opening just big enough to take Yarra's body. Inside, a narrow passage-way curved back a couple of yards and then opened out into a small, circular den about five feet in diameter. Years and years before, the entrance had been no more than a rabbit hole in the valley side. Generations of rabbits had tunnelled and warrened the chalky soil. Parts of it had collapsed and become enlarged. A pair of badgers, years before this moment, had taken it over and made it bigger. In the loose soil of the earth, thrown and eroded out of it, seeds had been dropped by birds, or had fallen from the coats of rabbit, badger and fox. Many vixens had cubbed there after the badgers left. Trees had sprouted and grown, and briars and thorns had seeded and flourished to make a screen that hid it. In all the years that the soldiers had used the plain, not one had ever found it. Yarra had found it when rabbit hunting along the ridge. Inside it was dry and warm, and Yarra meant to have her cubs there.

She had used it now for more than a week. During the day, when the soldiers were about in the village below, she liked to lie just outside the entrance, sleeping or dozing, and sometimes watching the far movements of men and vehicles.

She went into it now. In the half gloom she scraped at the loose chalk floor, then dropped to it and made herself comfortable. She lay, stretched flat out, her legs thrust away from her body, her head turned back on one shoulder. It was the way she liked to lie before sleeping.

Suddenly she twitched and stirred and gave a little growl. Inside her one of the cubs had kicked and moved. Yarra's head dropped. She licked at the line of her swollen dugs. The movement came again from inside her. She opened her great jaws in a yawning, silent unmasking of her fangs.

Within the next forty-eight hours Yarra was due to cub. That day was a Thurdsay.

*   *   *

When Smiler got back to Ford Cottage that evening, he made his usual cautious approach. It was a well-worn routine with him now. He first rode by the cottage on to the bridge to check for signs of life. Then he hid his bicycle in the copse behind the barn. From the kitchen garden he made a closer inspection of the house before slipping into the barn. When the light began to go, he always made a visit to the house to look at the letters which had been delivered while he was away. He left long before the postman called. He knew something of Mrs. Bagnall's habits now, too. She always came on a Wednesday morning. But sometimes if she was passing the cottage of an evening she would just look in to collect any mail for forwarding to Major Collingwood abroad. Smiler's chief concern was that there should come a day when the Major would send Mrs. Bagnall a postcard saying he was coming back. He knew, of course, that he might miss such a card when Mrs. Bagnall collected mail while he was away. But that was a chance he had to take.

What Smiler didn't know was that the Major was a man of uncertain routine. Sometimes he wrote to Mrs. Bagnall at the cottage, and sometimes he wrote to her at her own house. And what Smiler would have been very concerned to know on this evening was that Mrs. Bagnall that morning had received a card at her own house from the Major. It said that he and his wife – who was now in good health – were coming back on Sunday afternoon.

8

∽ A Happy Event – and Others ∽

Yarra had her cubs at six o'clock on Saturday evening. It had been a beautiful, warm April day. She lay most of the time on the patch of chalk just outside the cave entrance, blinking her eyes in the sun and watching the valley and the deserted village. Chiff-chaffs were calling in the tall trees. There was a bright sparkle of water by the road, where a spring rose to feed the little brook that ran through the village and away down the far valley. Two cuckoos exchanged their call signs most of the morning. Once a jay flighted up the valley side and sat in an ash above Yarra and scolded and shrieked at her. The movement in her belly went through her in slow waves and she changed her position frequently to find ease. She saw a Land Warden's patrol car move through the village twice during the day.

As the afternoon finally wore away Yarra got up and went into the gloom of the cave. Within an hour two cubs were born. They were little larger than kittens. Their eyes were shut and there was only the faintest shadow of marking on their grey bodies. Yarra cleaned herself, nuzzled the cubs close to her and licked and groomed them. They made pathetic mewing noises, their wet pelts starred with white chalk dust. After an hour they found her dugs. They butted and chewed at them for a while, finally found the coming milk, and began to suck. One cub was slightly larger than the other. This was a male. The other was a female.

Yarra lay happily with them, her head facing the cave entrance, her ears alert for any sound. When darkness came the cubs slept, cradled into the warm fur of her belly. Yarra caressed them with her muzzle and now and then licked at them. The restlessness had gone from her and she was at peace with the world.

With the coming of dawn light she was suddenly hungry. She stood up. The cubs sprawled away from her clumsily and then found one another. They huddled blindly together as Yarra left the cave.

She went up over the valley ridge on to the wide plain lands. Dawn was just coming up. On the wind from some distant farm came the sound of a cock crowing. A few early larks had risen and were filling the sky with song. Yarra trotted up the ridge to the higher reaches of the combe where it shallowed and finally merged with the long, undulating slopes of the high plain. Coming down wind to her Yarra suddenly caught a familiar scent. She froze and surveyed the ground. There was a slight movement in some tall grasses fifty yards ahead. Against the grass Yarra's keen eyes picked out a brown, white-mottled form, and she moved fast. Her body now was lighter than it had been, and there was a fierce joy in her that spurred her on as much as her hunger. A small fallow deer took to its feet ahead of her and went away like the wind. The deer, unlike a hare that would have twisted and doubled and tried every trick in the book, kept to a straight line, relying on speed.

Yarra ran it down within a hundred yards. She

leapt and hit it at top speed, bowling it over. The two animals rolled in a flurry of bodies and flying legs. When they came to a stop, Yarra's jaws were clamped across the deer's neck, her forepaws ripping at its throat. The deer died quickly and Yarra settled to eat.

She ate first into the belly, and then the meat from one of the deer's haunches, leaving most of the hide untouched. When she had finished and was full she left the carcase and turned back down the valley.

High above her, a carrion crow, marking her early morning sortie, had seen the chase and the kill. When she had started to eat he had planed down to a rock outcrop on the far slope to wait. As Yarra left he moved in to have his breakfast. A roving pair of rooks saw him and came down to the feast. They kept some distance away and darted in only now and then to snatch a morsel.

Yarra went down the valley fast, along the tank tracks. In one place turning tanks had scoured a great depression and had broken the earth crust deep enough for a small spring to burst through. The water bubbled up cold and clear. Yarra drank and then went up the steep valley side. She did not go straight back. She climbed out of the valley over the ridge and then moved along out of sight from the valley and the deserted village. When she was directly above the cave, she came back over the ridge, her silhouette low against the skyline, and dropped the few feet down to the cave.

Inside the cubs had become separated and were mewing and shivering. Yarra gathered them into the warmth and shelter of her belly fur. They soon found her dugs and began to suck. Yarra lay back as they fed and purred softly to herself.

*   *   *

Smiler was up early that morning, too. He had a quick breakfast of cheese and biscuits in the barn, washed himself in his bucket and then cycled off to Joe Ringer's cottage.

Joe was waiting for him by the van. It had double doors at the back. Inside the body was boarded off from the driving seat so that Smiler could not see if there was anything in it.

To Smiler's surprise Joe drove into Heytesbury and then took the road up to the plain past Danebury House. He stopped at the post-barred entry and made Smiler get out and raise the pole for him and lower it when he was through.

Back in the car Smiler said, "Mr. Ringer, we aren't allowed up here, are we?"

"Officially, no," said Joe with a wink. "But if a man obeyed every *no* there was going, he'd grow moss on himself in a month. Nothing to worry about, Johnny. I know every inch of this place. And on a Sunday I can tell you exactly where the Land Wardens will be and when. Just leave it to your Uncle Joe."

A bit later, when Smiler saw the notices about unexploded missiles, he asked about them.

"Eyewash," said Joe. "They pinched the land from the public and now they don't want 'em a-tramping over it. But the officers and their friends shoot and hunt over it. Think they'd do that if there was landmines and such like about? No, me lad, most you'll find is a few empty cartridge cases, some signal flare cannisters, and maybe a shell what ain't gone off when it should. You see anything you don't fancy – then leave it alone. I'll teach you all the tricks. Just leave it to your Uncle Joe."

Joe drove along the road for about a mile and then turned off down a rough track. Five hundred yards up the track was an abandoned Nissen hut with both ends missing. Joe drove the small van into the arched span of rusty corrugated iron and it was effectively hidden from sight.

A few minutes later they were moving over the long sweeps of a small plateau hunting for the lapwings' nests. Joe had a pair of field glasses and would sit for a while watching the birds in the air or for bird movement on the ground. The peewits nested right out in the open. When they came down from flight to their nests they always landed some way away and then moved through the long grass towards them. After watching an area for a while Joe had no trouble finding a few nests. Smiler was far from being an expert. Once he was standing looking about him for a nest when Joe said, "Go on, Johnny – you got a nest there."

"Where?" said Smiler.

"Right under yer nose," said Joe, pointing.

Smiler looked down. A yard in front of him on the almost bare ground he saw a shallow depression with three eggs in it. The eggs, green-and-brown-marked, blended perfectly against their background.

"Only one from each nest, mind," said Joe. "Mother Nature's a generous old gal – but she don't like greedy people."

They spent the whole morning looking for nests

and collecting the eggs, which Joe packed into a series of small boxes that he carried in his haversack. Once, he caught Smiler by the arm and pulled him down quickly.

"Stick your head between your legs and your hands under your arms – like this. And don't move!"

Smiler crouched on the ground as he was told. Not far away he heard the sound of a passing car.

"What is it, Mr. Ringer?" he asked, head between his knees.

"Land Warden. But he won't see us. Not at this distance. White face and hands is the give-away. Particularly if he happens to use his glasses. Right now we look just like a couple of big mole hills, lad. Leave it to your Uncle Joe."

The noise of the car died away into the distance. Joe raised his head and winked at Smiler.

"What would they do if we was caught?" asked Smiler.

Joe grinned. "String us up to the nearest tree, I don't think! No – all you'd get is a good talking-to. Unless your pockets was stuffed with pheasants or hares – or maybe peewees' eggs. But you don't want to worry about them old wardens. Come up here a few times with me and I'll learn you. Fancy, all this good poaching ground just given over to a pack of mostly city-bred soldiers what don't know a bull from a cow!"

Confident under the protection of Joe, Smiler thoroughly enjoyed the morning. Because he knew that Yarra was up here somewhere, he was tempted once or twice to tell Joe about her. But in the end he decided against it. If they should come across Yarra by accident he knew there would be no danger. Joe would know how to deal with the situation.

At mid-day they went back to the van to eat. Joe had loaded aboard cold pork sausages, hard-boiled eggs, a loaf of bread, cheese, ham and pickles, and two bottles of cider. They ate like princes with the wind singing through the grasses, the larks carolling above and little clouds of black gnats hovering above their heads. Smiler ate until he was full, but he was careful with the cider. He knew what it could do to him. And Joe's cider was *extra* strong.

After they had eaten, Joe decided that they had gathered enough eggs. They left them in the van. Joe said, "Now I'll show you where me old Daddy was brought up."

He then proceeded to take Smiler on almost the same line across country as Yarra had taken a few days before. But when they came down into the valley which held the deserted village, they hit it just above the church. Joe sat down on the slope and pointed to the shattered and derelict village.

"That's Imber village, Johnny. What's left of it. Prettiest village on the whole of the plain it was till the Army folk took it. See the church? My Grand-Mammy's buried there. And my Daddy grew up in a house that ain't standing no longer."

He sat, telling Smiler all about the place: how the Army, years before, when they had bought the great stretches of the plain for training, had left the people to live there. But when the Second World War came, the people all had to leave so that the village could be used for training American and British troops in the skills of house-to-house fighting. At the present time the same training still went on.

"See that big place down there across the road? That's Imber Court. That used to be the big house. Not a door, not a pane of glass left in it. Soldiers by day, rats by night. I tell you, when the folk had to leave this place, Johnny, it broke many a heart. Course, *they* very kindly out of their big military hearts lets 'em come back once or twice a year. Special treat to have a service in the church."

Joe shook his head and puffed at his pipe. Then, his eyes running up the narrow combe beyond the village and to the sky at the far end of it, he pointed and said, "See them?"

Smiler followed his pointing finger. High in the sky two large, broad-winged birds were circling slowly. Below a smaller, blacker bird was rising towards them. Suddenly the two higher birds dropped together towards the one below. They rolled and dived and swooped close about the smaller bird.

"What are they?" asked Smiler.

"Pair of buzzards and the feller below is a carrion crow. Them is a-fighting. Reckon down below there you'd find a dead rabbit or hare and they're arguing the toss about who's goin' to feed first. You keep your eyes open up here, Johnny, and you'll see lots of things. I'll teach you."

Smiler said, "It must've been nice living up here."

"Well, that's what comes of fightin' and having wars. And people poking their noses into other people's business, and other folks likin' to dress up in uniforms and all that rigmarole." Joe lay back and laughed. "Know somethin', Johnny? A real secret? They took me for the Army a long time back. But they couldn't hold me. I upped and run, and they never caught me. Never. I'm a deserter of long standin' – and that's the way I'm going to be for the rest of me life. And you're the first one I ever told, Johnny."

"Oh, I won't tell anyone, Mr. Ringer."

"Don't suppose it would matter much after all this time if you did, Johnny. And don't keep givin' me that Mr. Ringer bit. I'm Joe to me friends."

After a while they made their way back to the van. But Joe did not drive off right away. He looked at his watch and made Smiler listen with him until they heard the sound of a Land-Rover passing on the road which they had left that morning.

"Regular as clockwork mostly they is, them Wardens," said Joe. "Time your watch to 'em."

A few minutes later they were driving back along the road and Joe was promising that he would bring Smiler up to the plain again very soon.

"We'll take the ferrets and nets up and have a go for the rabbits. Set a few traps for hares maybe – though they ain't much eatin' at this time of year. Oh, I'll show you around this place, me lad, so you'll know it like the back of your hand. Keep your ears and eyes open and not a soul will worry you. Yes, just you leave it to your Uncle Joe."

Because Joe made him stop and have supper in his cottage, Smiler was late getting back to Ford Cottage.

He cycled back through the gloaming in a very happy state of mind. At the river bridge over the Wylye he stopped and looked at the water. Joe had promised to teach him all about trout fishing – in season and out. "No findanglin' about with flies. You want a big trout – then you want a big worm on the hook." He was going to show him his way around the plain, too. The thought of the plain gave Smiler a nice, warm, excited feeling. It was so big and wild and full of life. Yarra was up there, too. He liked the thought of that. At supper, in a roundabout way, he had brought up the subject of Yarra. What, he had asked Joe, would he do if he met the cheetah, say, on the plain? Joe had said, "Just stand your ground, lad. Stand your ground and stare it out. She'd go. Specially with a lad of your size. Now, if you was a little nipper . . . well, that might be different. But mostly all animals want nothing to do with humans. Give 'em the chance and they're away. You know what? I stared out a bull once. Real ugly he acted, too, for a bit, but I stared him out. Went away with his tail between his legs. It's the human eye, you see. Animals – 'ceptin' domestic ones – can't stand human eyes. Or," he laughed, draining his glass of cider, "– maybe it's just the faces they can't stand."

As Smiler came down the hill from Sutton Veny towards the river, he passed Lodge Cottage. The lights were showing behind the sitting-room curtains. Pat Bagnall was probably in there watching television. He had been into Woolworth's since he had spoken to her there, but she was not behind the electrical counter. So, he guessed, she must have got herself some new job.

Happy, though tired, Smiler free wheeled down the hill, past Ford Cottage and across the bridge, as he always did, to give it a look over before venturing in. Within a few seconds his happiness had gone.

As he drew level with the courtyard entrance he

knew that his shelter had been taken from him. It was still light enough for him to see a car parked in the courtyard. The big five-barred gate was unpadlocked and open. From the kitchen window a light shone out. He rode to the bridge, propped himself on his bike against the parapet and looked at the front of the house. The dining-room window was dark, but there was a light showing through the sitting-room window, and another from the main bedroom. He guessed at once what had happened. Major and Mrs. Collingwood were back!

Smiler sat on his cycle and stared at the house. Dismay filled him and he groaned quietly to himself, "Oh, Crikey! Oh, Holy, Smoking Crikeys!"

At that moment from the dark sky above a fat drop of rain splashed on to Smiler's hand. He looked up. A quick splatter of heavy drops fell on his face as the first of a series of fierce April rainstorms swept through the river valley. In two minutes the rain was lashing down, churning up the surface of the river and sending Smiler racing for shelter – for the only shelter he knew.

He cycled back up the hill, hid his bicycle in the coppice and then hurried back around the rear of the barn. He surveyed the rain-blurred yard for a second or two and then slipped round and into the barn. Standing at the dusty window in the loft he stripped off his anorak and watched the house. For the moment all he could think of was that *they* were back. What was he going to do? WHAT WAS HE GOING TO DO? Then, pulling himself together, he began to give himself a good talking-to. Samuel M., he said, stop trembling and being scared. You've taken a little water aboard, but you aren't sunk yet by a long shot. Just think it all out! Nice and cool! No panic! NO PANIC! JUST THINK!

He sat down on a bale of hay and began to think.

* * *

Inside Ford Cottage Major Collingwood was in the sitting-room by himself having his coffee after a late supper. His wife was upstairs doing something in their bedroom. He got up and went to the corner cupboard where the drinks were kept. He had had a long travelling day and he felt like a glass of brandy with his coffee. As he poured himself the brandy, his eye fell on the box of cigars where Smiler had lodged his letter of apology. The sight of the box made him wonder if he would celebrate his home-coming with a cigar. He reached out for the box, touched its lid, and then changed his mind. He did not often smoke cigars, keeping them mostly for his guests. No, a little extra brandy would perhaps be a better celebration. He lifted the bottle and added more brandy to his glass.

Upstairs Mrs. Collingwood went into the bathroom to set out fresh towels which she had taken from the airing cupboard. As she drew the curtains she noticed some small brown stains and frowned to herself. They looked like rust marks, she thought. But how could curtains go rusty? She puzzled over it for a moment and then put it out of her mind. Anyway, she had long ago promised to treat herself to a new pair of curtains for the bathroom.

Downstairs Major Collingwood sat contentedly with his brandy and coffee. He was happy because he was home and even happier because his wife was fully recovered. His eye fell on the sixpenny bottle on the bookshelf. It looked just the same as when he had left it – which it should have done because Smiler had conscientiously replaced all the sixpences he had borrowed. When it was full, the Major promised himself, he would take the money and buy a present as a surprise for his wife. It was a generous decision because he had been really saving up to buy himself a new fly-fishing rod.

Hearing the rain pelting down outside he told himself that he really must go out and put the car in the barn garage. But then he felt so comfortable that he decided against it. A little rain wouldn't hurt the car for one night. In fact it would wash it clean.

*   *   *

While Major and Mrs. Collingwood were comfortably installed in the cottage, Smiler lay on his hay and did a lot of thinking. His first panic had long gone and he was being very practical. When Smiler wanted to he could really think a problem right through. By the time he fell asleep he knew just exactly what had to be done. It was going to take a little bit of careful handling, but he was sure that he was man enough for the task. He slept. In the hay close to his head, deeply buried, was the alarm clock which he had set for five o'clock. He had to be away in the morning long before there was any chance that the Collingwoods would be awake.

*   *   *

In her den, on the hillside above Imber, Yarra slept

with her cubs. All night the rain-storms swept south-west across the plain. Once Yarra woke to find the cubs sucking at her. She nosed at them. Their pelts now were dry and soft and silky with a fine fuzz of hair. Outside she could hear the gurgle and splash of storm water cascading over the lip of the cave entrance to the bare chalk below. Down in the village a marauding old dog fox, hungry enough to dare the weather, turned into the deserted ground floor of Imber Court to see if he could pick up an unwary mouse or rat. In a corner of one of the bare rooms he found half a corned-beef sandwich left there two days before by a soldier. The fox ate it with relish.

9

✍ A Change of Lodgings ✍

The alarm clock woke Smiler. Outside the noise of
the night's rain was gone. He got up and set about
his plan of evacuation. He gathered all his spare
clothes into a bundle and tied it with string so that
he could sling it on his back. He put his tin with his
money in his anorak pocket. He had saved almost
twenty pounds by now. The alarm clock and a few
other odds and ends he tucked inside his anorak.
Keeping the light of his bicycle lamp low he tidied
up the loft. There was nothing he could do about the
transistor set, so he left it in full view on a hay bale.
Down below he put away the bucket he had used
for washing. Then, not without some sadness
because he had come to think of it as home, he left
the barn.

He got the bicycle and drove down to the stone
bridge. He stopped for a moment and looked back
at the black bulk of the cottage where Major and Mrs.
Collingwood were sleeping soundly. Some time, he
thought, the Major would find his letter, the
transistor set, and miss the bicycle. What would he
do then? Report to the police? Or just shrug his
shoulders. After all, it wasn't much of a bicycle.
Smiler had already had to buy two new tyres for it.
Anyway, thought Smiler, there was nothing he
could do about it except some day send the Major
the price of a replacement bicycle. Yes, that's what
he would do. He certainly didn't want to dip into

his savings right now to do it. At any moment he might be in real need of money if he had to make a fast get-away to some far place.

He pushed his bicycle up the hill and began to ride slowly to work. He reached Danebury House in good time as he had intended. He knew the habits of the house well now. Mrs. Lakey never appeared out of the house before half-past seven.

Tonks met him at the gate with a welcome bark, but Smiler gave him a sharp word of warning and Tonks was obediently quiet. He rode round to the stable and put all his stuff up into the loft under a bale of straw. Then he went up to the garden and let the Twelve Apostles out into their run, picked up the eggs which had been laid overnight, and took them down to the kitchen.

While he was there Mrs. Lakey came in. She gave him an odd look and said, "You're around early this morning, Boy. Bad conscience or bad dreams, or both?"

"It was all that rain, Mrs. Lakey. I couldn't sleep."

"At your age you should sleep through a hurricane."

She gave him his coffee and then Smiler went about his morning jobs. Although he did his work well his mind wasn't really on it. Last night in making his plans he had been confident, but now as the moment for putting them into action grew nearer and nearer he wasn't so sure about them. People liked you and were friendly to you, and all that. But when it came to doing a real favour – and without asking too many questions. . . . Well, that was a horse of a different colour. However, he couldn't be gloomy for long. It was such a splendid morning after the rain. The April sun was a burnished ball in the sky. The rooks were cawing their heads off in their nesting colony at the top of the roadside elms. Blackbirds and thrushes were filling the air with riotous song and the paddock, when he exercised the dogs, was a sheet of green enamel. A wren had nested in the stable and flitted fussily around while Smiler was mucking it out. Half-way through the morning Lemon Drop and Captain Black's Alsatian had a fight and Smiler had to break it up. Outdoor work had made him strong now and he held them apart easily, giving them both a good talking-to.

At mid-day Miss Milly gave him boiled beef and carrots and his favourite jam roll with custard. When she asked him what he had done on his Sunday off he felt that it was better to say he'd gone for a bike ride, rather than tell her about Joe and the peewees' eggs. But she gave him an awkward moment when she said, "I saw you come from my bedroom window this morning, Johnny. What on earth was all that stuff on your back?"

"Stuff, Miss Milly?"

Miss Milly grinned. "Yes, stuff, Johnny. A big package on your back."

Smiler thought fast. "Oh, that, Miss Milly. That's some stuff my auntie wants me to take to the cleaners in Warminster on the way back."

"You don't leave till half-past five, Johnny. They'll be shut." Smiler's working time had been extended with the lengthening evenings.

"Not till six, Miss Milly. I can just make it."

Miss Milly shook her head. "I don't want you

cycling like a mad thing up that dangerous main road." She winked at him. "Mrs. Lakey's taking Bacon to be shoed at four. You leave at five. But keep it to yourself, Johnny, or there will be considerable dissension between ever-loving sisters."

"Thank you, Miss Milly."

So Smiler left at five, laden with his household goods, to face the most testing part of the day.

He rode up the valley to Joe's cottage and left his bicycle and belongings just inside the garden gate. He went round the back of the cottage and found Joe repainting the faded sign on the side of his green van. The sign read – JOS. RINGER – DEALER – ALL GOODS HANDLED – LOWEST PRICES. Joe had got as far as the word PRICES.

He turned and saw Smiler and paint dripped off his brush to the yard floor.

He grinned and said, "Hullo, Johnny. Finished for the day?"

"Yes, Mr. Ringer."

Joe frowned. "Joe it is and Joe it must stay." He turned and pointed to the fresh white sign. "Eye-catcher, eh? Lowest Prices – know what that means? If *they* got something to sell – I pays the lowest prices. But if *they* wants something from me . . . well, then if I don't like their face *they* pays the highest prices. Economics, that is. What you hoppin' about from one leg to the other for?"

"I'm all right, Joe."

"Then why you lookin' as though you'd lost a shilling and found threepence?"

Smiler hesitated for a moment and then decided to plunge. "I got a bit of a problem, Joe."

"We all have, lad. Is it economic, personal, or

136

religious? Help offered for all but the last. Like a glass of cider to loosen your tongue?"

"No thank you, Joe."

"Then I will – to give me strength. From the look of your face you must have murdered the Lord Mayor of London. Here, hold this brush."

Joe handed the brush to Smiler and went to the house. He returned with the cider jar and an old chipped china mug. He filled the mug and sat down on a box.

"Now then, Johnny me lad. Let's hear your problem."

Smiler hesitated for a moment and then he blurted out, "I got to find lodgings, Joe. And . . . and . . . I thought you might be able to help me."

Joe grinned. "Seeing as we're friends, and that's what friends is for, eh? Helping one another. But don't let's give the old horse a good gallop afore we knows where we're goin'. What you want lodgings for? You got a perfectly good auntie over at Crockerton. Don't tell me you've had an up-and-downer with her?"

"No, we haven't quarrelled. It just is . . . well . . ." Smiler didn't like telling a lie to Joe, but for safety's sake he had to. "Well, she's gone away. This morning. And she won't be back for a month. More maybe. And she thought it would be better if I found lodgings near the job. I could pay about two pounds a week. And if wanted give a hand around the place. And then –"

"Whoa!" cried Joe. "Rein her in a bit! Your auntie's gone off this morning?"

"That's right."

"Why, me lad?"

"Her sister's very sick. Down in . . . in Bristol."

Joe considered this and said slyly, "You sure it's Bristol and not, say, Yarmouth?"

"It's Bristol. She's very old and very sick, this sister. She's my auntie, too." Smiler was rather pleased with this last touch.

"Naturally," said Joe. "And your aunt only heard about this this morning and had to pack her gear and hump it away to Bristol?"

"Yes."

"Short notice, eh? But then sisters is always inconsiderate to one another – they tell me. Who's going to look after Hillside Bungalow?"

"The woman next door."

"As a good neighbour should. You'll go there now and then to run an eye over it, like?"

"Most week-ends, yes."

Joe finished his mug of cider and refilled it. He sat considering Smiler very closely, his face, brown as polished oak, half-thoughtful, half-smiling.

Then he said, "You want to give me a straight answer to a straight question, Johnny?"

"Of course, Mr. Ring – . . . I mean, Joe."

"Well, then Johnny, me lad, you listen carefully. I'm a man as likes to keep his own business to hisself. I make a living and the ways I do it ain't always by the book. But I haven't never done anything really bad. You know what I mean by that?"

"I think so, Joe."

"You'd better *know* so, Johnny. By really bad I means something you wake up and think about in the night – and you know it was really bad and you

138

wish you'd never done it. You get what I mean, Johnny?"

"I think so, Joe."

"I mean like I wouldn't want to help anyone to find lodgings that had, say, pinched money out of the church box, or knocked off the till in a shop, or had been some kind of tearaway who'd think nothing, say, of bundling a poor old lady off a pavement and pinching her handbag. Them's the kind I wouldn't help. So give me a straight answer, Johnny. You ever done anything like that?"

Smiler hesitated. He liked Joe and he wasn't going to lie to him over this – not even to get a good lodgings.

He said, "I pinched a few comic books sometimes. And, maybe, nicked a bottle of milk or a bar of chocolate that just happened to be there. But I didn't ever do anything bad like you said. Not ever. Cross me throat and hope to die!" He pulled the edge of his hand across his neck.

Joe nodded. "Just like I thought." He stood up. "Well then, about these lodgings. I got to admit that they're hard to come by. Specially at the price you're offerin'. But it just so happens that I like a bit of young company about the place. And, it just so happens that there's two bedrooms here and I only uses one. And, it just so happens, Johnny me lad, that not bein' hard up for an odd penny I ain't out to make a profit from a friend – so you can have the room for a quid a week. Make your own bed, keep your room tidy, help in the house – and the yard! And neither of us ask awkward questions of the other when we can see as how they ain't in place. Suit you?"

Delighted, Smiler cried, "Oh, thank you, Mr. Ringer!"

Joe frowned. " 'Nother thing. Every time you call me Mr. Ringer you muck out the pig pen. Joe it is."

"I won't forget, Joe."

"Don't mind if you do now and then – that pig pen's an awful chore. Now then, pop out and get your bike and your stuff. I seed you comin' along the lane humped up like a bloomin' camel. And Johnny, another thing."

"Yes?"

"I don't think as I would mention your change of address to Mrs. Lakey and Miss Milly. They mightn't think I was a fit and proper person for you to lodge with."

"Of course they would. You're super."

"All the same. Don't let on. What women don't know won't worry 'em. Though I must say, they usually finds out in the end. Bring your stuff in, and then we'll go get ourselves a couple of fat trout for supper."

*   *   *

At the time when Smiler was taking his belongings into Joe's cottage Yarra was coming out of her den on the hillside. Imber village had been full of training soldiers all day and they had stayed rather later than they usually did. Yarra, too wise now to risk showing herself when there were human beings about, had kept in the den or at its mouth all day. When the cubs were full of milk and sleeping, she had lain half in and half out of the entrance watching the valley and the village below. All day there had been a movement of tanks and trucks through the place, the crackle of blank ammunition being fired and, now and again, a green or red flare would burst in the bright air and drift earthwards with a plume of tawny smoke rising from it. Higher up the combe a squad of soldiers had been firing two-inch mortar bombs over the ridge at an unseen target. Once a badly aimed mortar bomb had exploded on the ridge thirty yards behind the cave. It had shaken loose chalk and small stones from the roof. Yarra, touchy now that she had young to protect, had grown angry and hungry. But she would not leave the den until the men had gone from the village.

When at last the valley and the village were peaceful, Yarra left the cave. She moved swiftly up on to the ridge and then passed along it just below the skyline. The dry, tawny grasses of winter were marked now with new growths. Trefoils and small harebells showed their blossoms on the rabbit-bitten bare patches. Hungry, Yarra's keen eyes marked every movement around her: the flight of an early bee; the dance of a small hatch of flies above a rain pool; the flirt of wing and the scut of a rabbit's tail. But she wasn't interested in a rabbit. She wanted more substantial game.

High above Yarra three pairs of eyes watched her. The two circling buzzards, lazing aloft on a rising thermal current, saw her and drifted in her wake. While they mostly hunted for themselves, taking small birds, rodents and young rabbits, they were not too proud to feast at the remains of another animal's table. In the past Yarra had provided them with free hare and deer leftovers. So they followed her, spiralling round and round, waiting for her to make a kill.

The carrion crow, an ancient, weathered bird of the plains, watched Yarra too. Sliding across wind above her, but far below the buzzards, he turned a neat somersault and came down under the stiff breeze to perch on a solitary thorn that marked the valley ridge a few hundred yards from the cave. The crow knew the buzzards were watching Yarra's movements. He knew that if she made a kill they would give him no peace to take a supper from the leavings. It was not that he was afraid of them; but they were big, flappy-winged birds. They would – as they had often done – come sailing down above him, rolling and mewing a few feet above his head and upsetting him. This evening the crow felt in the mood for a more peaceful meal. And at this time of the year he knew where to find one. This was the time of the year when Nature began to spread her banquet for the predators. Nests were filling with young birds. The rabbit holes and warrens held young. The hare forms in the young bracken and tall grasses sheltered leverets, and almost every dead mole hill held a mouse's nest that could be dug out. The carrion crow knew that any hole or cranny was likely to hold something good to eat.

For many days now he had seen Yarra coming out of her cave entrance and he was curious. He watched her move away into the distant folds of the plain and then he flapped slowly down to settle on an ash outside the entrance.

He cocked his head and listened for any sound from the cave. He could hear nothing because the cubs were deep in milk-gorged sleep. He sat there for ten minutes and considered the entrance. It was bigger than most he knew. He was a wise old bird and realized that once inside a rabbit hole there was little chance of using wings for flight. All he would have was his great black beak and claws to defend himself. He considered the cave entrance for a while, the westering sun striking turquoise and purple sheens from the long feathers of his great square tail. He uttered a bad-tempered *kwaarp*, and then flew down to the cave entrance. Slowly he began to stalk inside, jerking his great head about, on the alert for the slightest sound or movement. He turned the corner of the small tunnel run and was faced with the gloom of the cave itself. Although a fair amount of light seeped through into the cave, the crow stood there for a while until his eyes grew accustomed to the gloom. After a moment or two, the crow saw a slight movement at the back of the cave as one of the cubs stirred in its sleep. The crow moved forward, deliberately, cautiously, step by step, his great black beak held ready to thrust. One blow with his beak would break and pierce the skull of a young rabbit or kitten.

On the plain Yarra put up a hare from a small hollow filled with dead bracken drift. One of the buzzards high above saw the movement of the hare and the fast take-off of Yarra as she went after it. The buzzard mewed loudly, calling to its mate. The other buzzard swung downwind to close formation. The buzzards hung together, swinging round in a tight circle, watching the hunt.

Yarra closed rapidly with the hare, which was one she had chased before. It was a big, well-fleshed animal that knew its way around the plains. Before, it had escaped from Yarra by diving under a derelict tank where she could not reach it. But this time there was no such refuge in sight. The hare raced away with ears and eyes laid back. He could see Yarra following and gaining on him, no matter how much he swerved and switched, side-jumped and doubled and twisted. Yarra overhauled him fast. When she was three feet from him she went into her killing leap. The hare saw Yarra spring from the ground behind him. Desperate, he produced the only trick he had to offer. As Yarra took off – the hare stopped dead in his tracks. One moment he was going at top speed and the next he was crouched motionless in the grass. Yarra sailed right over the top of him, overshooting him by a yard.

The hare flashed round and was away. Yarra, angry and hungry, screwed sideways as she landed, her talons tearing up grass and soil. In fifty yards she was on his tail again – and this time she did not miss.

The buzzards above saw her make her kill, mewed excitedly to one another, and began to drift lower on the evening wind.

In the cave on the hillside the carrion crow was now standing two feet from the cubs. He could see them clearly. Although he had never seen anything like Yarra before, the cubs were no surprise to him. He had killed many litters of wild-cat kittens. These were kittens, young and tender.

He waddled forward, beak poised for the kill. As he did so, a stone in the roof, loosened by the mortar bomb during the day, dropped from its place and thudded to the ground behind him. The crow turned with a jump and a flap of his wings.

He faced the cave entrance warily. After a while his tenseness faded. He turned and moved again towards the cubs. They were lying a little separated and the crow instinctively chose the larger for his kill.

He stood a foot from it, lowered his head and sharp beak and prepared to jump in and thrust with all his power. At that instant a shadow passed over the back wall of the cave.

The crow swung round to face Yarra as she came quickly into the cave, carrying a large hare in her mouth.

It was the last thing the carrion crow ever saw. Yarra dropped the hare and leapt for him. Her jaws took him under the neck as he tried to fly up. Holding him, she killed him and then, still gripping him in her teeth, shook and swung him about so that long black primary and small breast feathers floated about the cave. Then she dropped him and went to the cubs, waking them as she nosed and muzzled and licked them. They had been saved because, as Yarra had settled on the grass to eat her kill, a new instinct in her had suddenly been born, an instinct which was soon to become a maternal habit – the instinct to take food back to her lair for the cubs. She had brought the hare back to share with her young, though it was going to be many days yet before they would be ready for solid food.

*　　*　　*

At Ford Cottage Major Collingwood came into the kitchen. He had been pottering around the garden and barn. It was now time for him to tidy himself up before having dinner. He was a kind, pleasant-looking man, his dark hair well streaked with grey over the ears.

He said to his wife, who was mixing up eggs to make an omelette, "You know, love – some blighter's pinched that old bike from the barn."

Mrs. Collingwood smiled and said, "Then you should be glad. It was just a load of old junk. And you'd better get cleaned up. Omelettes won't wait for anyone – not even retired Army majors."

"It's funny," said the Major. "Not just about the bike. But I got a funny feeling in the barn."

"Indigestion?" Mrs. Collingwood smiled and cocked an eyebrow at him.

"No, my dear. But I'm pleased to see that you are now back in all your former *rude* health."

"What kind of feeling then?"

"As though something's been about."

"You mean a ghost?"

"No. Somebody. I just get that feeling."

"Well, then, perhaps it's the one who had the sardines because I'm quite sure Mrs. Bagnall would never have taken them."

"You mean you've missed sardines? From in here?"

"Either that. Or I miscounted before we went away. Six tins, I thought. Now there're only three."

"How could you possibly remember?"

"A woman does. Now go and get cleaned up. I told you –"

"That an omelette, like Time, waits for no man."

Major Collingwood went upstairs looking thoughtful and a little puzzled. And Major Collingwood, since he had done all his service in the Royal Corps of Military Police, was the kind of man who rather enjoyed a puzzle or a mystery. Since his wife had now mentioned the marks on the bathroom curtain, he studied them carefully before beginning to tidy himself up.

* * *

The cause of Major Collingwood's puzzlement was at that moment sitting with Joe in his kitchen having supper. Each of them was enjoying a grilled brown trout from the River Wylye which ran along the end of the field below Joe's cottage. Although it was a few days before the trout fishing season opened officially, it would have made no difference to Joe if there had been two months or more to go.

An hour before he had given Smiler his first experience of poaching trout. They had gone down to the river at the end of the field. Here, across the stream, was a set of hatches – like large wooden doors – that could be raised or lowered to regulate the flow of water to the weir pool below.

They sat on the hatchway run above the top of the pool and Joe tied a hook on the end of a spool of nylon line, which had a small stick through the centre of it. He showed Smiler the right knot to use. A half-blood knot, he called it. Then he threaded several worms on to the hook and clipped a heavy lead weight on to the line three feet above the hook.

They sat on the hatchway planks and Joe dropped the hooked, baited and weighted line into the water. He paid it out very gently as the bottom current took the lead weight slowly downstream along the river bed.

"You sits here like this, Johnny me lad," said

Joe. "And it being still light you looks all innocent and enjoyin' the view. Then, if'n a river keeper shows up, or one of the gents what has fishin' rights, you just lets go the spool gentle. The whole lot sinks and you come back next day and fish it out. Always lookin' innocent and enjoyin' the view is important."

As he spoke he paid out line slowly, keeping a slight tension on it through his fingers.

"But if you is left in peace, you just pays away the line like this. Sooner or later one of them big trout below the hatch what the fishing gents can't ever get with their little bitty flies, will go for the worms. And, Johnny me lad, let 'em go for 'em you must. Even when you feel 'em. Let 'em take it all. No striking like the fly-fisher folk do. That old trout'll hook himself in no time. Lke this one! Whoa!"

The line in Joe's hand suddenly streaked away and Joe let it run for a moment or two from the spool. Downstream a fish suddenly broke water in a great silvery jump. Joe held the line firm now, and the trout dived and darted all over the pool for a while. Then Joe began to haul the fish in without any finesse and lifted it up to the hatch on the end of the line.

"Always use a good, strong nylon line. Six or eight pounds breaking strain. The old trout won't worry about the thickness of the line if'n there's a bunch of worms on the end."

He smacked the head of the trout across a wooden post of the hatch opening, unhooked it, and dropped it into his pocket. He said, "Now then, you have a go. I've got my supper."

He made Smiler thread fresh worms on the hook.

Smiler paid out the line as Joe had shown him. Within five minutes he had caught his supper. It was a beautiful brown trout, firm flanked, and flecked with lovely red and yellow spots.

"Kill 'un quick. That's a kindness some of these fancy fishers don't always bother about. That's a nice fish. Pound and half. It'll eat like nothing you've ever tasted before. Leave it to Uncle Joe. You'll see."

Later, Smiler sat with Joe in his new lodgings, the both of them eating grilled trout and drinking cider (Smiler being very careful how much he took, and Joe treating it like water). As he washed up the supper things for Joe afterwards, Smiler remembered how worried he had been that morning about how it would all turn out. And it couldn't have turned out better! It just showed that it did no good to worry too much about things that *might* happen. Though what he would have done without Joe, he just didn't know. Samuel M., he said, don't you ever forget what a good sort Joe is . . . and one day. . . . Well, one day you've got to find some way of paying Joe back. Say, for instance, you got really rich. Rolling in it, because you invented something that was bringing in thousands. . . . Well then, you could buy Joe a new van. . . . Yes, that was it. A new van.

He stood there day-dreaming over the washing up. There wasn't a cloud on his horizon. In five or six more months his father would be back.

*   *   *

While Smiler day-dreamed, Major Collingwood and his wife were having their after dinner coffee. The

Major went to get himself a glass of brandy. His wife said she did not want one. This time, seeing the cigar box and feeling extra happy to be back and that his wife was in such *rude* health and, because, after all, there was no place quite like home – particularly when you had a wife like Mrs. Collingwood – he told himself that he jolly well would have a cigar with his brandy.

So, he opened the cigar box and found Smiler's letter. As he looked down at it, the telephone began to ring in the hallway. Mrs. Collingwood went to answer it. Major Collingwood stood there, reading Smiler's letter.

10

∽ *Enquiries Are Being Made* ∽

Major Collingwood liked the tone of the letter. Whoever "Hunted" was, he was a decent sort of chap with some kind of conscience. But if he liked the letter, he also liked mysteries even better. Being retired he had plenty of time on his hands. He had already found the transistor set in the barn, and had said nothing to his wife. The letter offered him a little detection work which he felt might fill many a long hour. However, because he knew his wife wouldn't like the idea that someone had used the house while they were away – it might make her nervous and upset – he decided for the moment to say nothing to her.

He slipped the letter into his pocket before she came back from the hall, and sat down with his brandy and cigar. He had decided that he was going to trace *Mr. Hunted*, quietly on his own. When he found him . . . well, then he would decide what to do.

When his wife came back, she said, "That was the Cokes. They want us to go to dinner next Friday."

"Splendid," the Major said. His friend Mr. Coke was a retired Chief Constable who still kept in very close touch with all police affairs and criminal incidents in the area. He could have an interesting chat with him without giving his private mystery away.

When he went up to bed that night, the Major took a closer look at the bathroom curtain, and then a closer look at the contents of the bathroom cabinet. He smiled to himself. If you used dark brown hair dye it could only be to make your hair darker, surely? But if you used sun-tan stuff before summer came. . . . Well, that was interesting now, wasn't it? He would have to think that one out.

*　　*　　*

The next morning Smiler rode to work as happy as a lark. He was so light-hearted, in fact, that he had to sing aloud to himself. Smiler had a good voice and he sang a favourite ditty of his father.

> *"Go tell Aunt Rhody,*
> *Go tell Aunt Rhody,*
> *Go tell Aunt Rhody,*
> *The old grey goose is dead.*
>
> *The one that she's been a-savin',*
> *The one that she's been a-savin',*
> *The one that she's been a-savin',*
> *To make a feather bed."*

Some days later Joe heard him singing one of his songs, and Joe joined in. At some time in his life Joe had been to America and he taught Smiler lots of new songs. Sometimes of an evening they would have a concert just for themselves, and Joe would bang away on an old piano he'd bought for five pounds and Smiler would sing his head off.

But this morning Smiler was singing just for himself because of the happiness inside him. He went about his work singing and whistling. Every time Miss Milly heard him outside she would stop what she was doing and smile and nod. Sometimes, if she knew the tune, she would go on with her work, humming it to herself. Only Mrs. Lakey said to herself, "That Boy's worse than having a canary about the place." But even she was pleased because the only thing with a long face she liked was a horse.

It was the beginning of two months of bliss for Smiler. April ran into May and early Summer smiled on the valleys and plains. Marsh marigolds, frogbit, and water crowfoot flourished on the pond in the paddock. The primroses went and the blue-bells came. Bryony wreathed up the hedges and the wild garlic flourished under the trees by the river. The trout and graylings grew fat on flies, nymphs and caddis grubs. The fledglings feathered up and felt an urge in their wings that made them restless in their overcrowded nests. The cuckoo pints un-furled their green sheaths and attracted small insects to crawl about over their stigmas and pollinate them. In the hedgerows, the real cuckoos had long deposited their eggs in other birds' nests.

Up on the plain Yarra looked after her cubs and hunted for them. Their eyes opened and their pelts began to take on the characteristic cheetah markings. Yarra brought them small birds, mice, shrews, once or twice a green lizard, and rabbits and hares. They grew stronger and steadier on their feet but still stayed within the cave. When they were bored they fought one another. When fighting bored them, the male would sometimes explore towards the mouth of the cave. Whenever Yarra saw him doing this she would cuff him back.

Smiler began to know the plain, too, for Joe often now took him up there poaching. Sometimes of an evening, for the evenings had now grown long with daylight, Smiler would go up on the plain by himself. He knew the movements of the Land Wardens' Land-Rovers now and easily avoided them. He came to learn every dip and slope, every hollow and valley-side for miles around the deserted village of Imber. He had, too, his own ways of going on to the plain, avoiding the Vedette entrances. Since he now lived with Joe he could walk from Joe's cottage to Imber in little over an hour.

Often when Smiler went up to the plain he took with him Joe's field glasses. He loved to lie just below some ridge-top and watch the wild sweeps of country. Through the glasses he came to know the movements of many of the animals. He knew the foxes and the buzzards and, on the fringe of the plain not far above Danebury House, he knew a badger's set. Watching late into the dusk one day, he had seen the old boar badger come out for his night's foraging.

But the thing that really excited Smiler – and something he had never told Joe about – was that he had three times seen Yarra. The real reason he had not told Joe about it was that about four times a week Joe went down for the evening to the Angel Inn at Heytesbury. When Joe took too much cider aboard he had a habit of slipping the guard on his tongue. Smiler didn't want him to talk about Yarra in the Angel because that would mean a search and hunting party going up for her. Smiler didn't want her caught. Her freedom had somehow become linked with his own freedom. He felt in a funny way that it would be dead unlucky for him if he ever betrayed her.

He first saw her through his glasses on a Sunday evening. She was some way from Imber, hunting. He picked her up as she came quickly over the skyline. For five minutes he watched her quarter and hunt along a slope a mile from him. She took a hare and he saw for the first time in his life the tremendous turn of speed cheetahs can produce. The second time she was much closer to him. He was sitting up on one of the high-stilted observation platforms which the Army used for soldiers to watch the fall of shot around tank targets. It was on the side of the valley that ran eastwards from Imber. In the valley bottom was the small brook that came down through the village. The stream had almost died out to a trickle now as its spring source slowly fell off. But there were still a few pools along its length. Yarra came down to the brook to drink not a hundred yards from him. She lapped like a cat for a while. Then she turned and disappeared behind the trees that fringed the road leading to Imber.

The third time he saw her was from the farm buildings at the back of Imber Court. He was watching the pair of buzzards circling over a narrow combe that ran up to the north from the village. One of them suddenly mewed and planed down-wards out of sight beyond the steep valley-side. The other buzzard followed. As Smiler brought his glasses down, following the birds, he saw Yarra come quickly over the ridge crest.

She came a few yards down the steep side and then disappeared behind a leafy screen of ash and alder trees. Smiler moved up the opposite side of the valley and examined the trees through his glasses. His observation being now from a different angle, he saw at once the tunnel entrance behind the trees. He watched it for an hour and there was no sign of Yarra. He guessed that it was probably her resting place or den, and made a note to himself to keep well away from it. There was plenty of room for both of them on the plain.

So the days passed for Smiler and Yarra. Smiler worked at Danebury, grew stronger and brown-tanned over his freckles so that he needed no artificial sun-tan. But every few weeks he had to dye his hair. (When it wanted cutting Joe would do it for him in the yard.) He always dyed his hair on an evening when Joe was down at the Angel, and he was very careful to clear up all signs of his operation afterwards. And he now knew where Pat Bagnall was working. He had gone into the food market in Warminster to get some supplies for Joe – and there she was sitting at a check-out point! There were a lot of people waiting to pay for their goods so he only had a brief talk with her. He met her again one Sunday morning when he was down at the river getting a couple of trout for his and Joe's evening meal. She had come down for a ride with her father, the river-keeper. He was doing something to the hatches lower down river.

Smiler was glad to hear this because he already had two fat trout hidden in the bushes not four yards from them.

Although he liked her, he didn't care for the direct way she put personal questions.

She wanted to know where he lived.

Smiler nodded his head across the fields to

Joe's cottage. "Over there – with my uncle, Joe Ringer."

Pat laughed. "My dad knows him all right. Fancy you being related. Hope you don't carry on like he does sometimes. Dad says he's worse than otter or heron where fish is concerned."

"Uncle Joe's all right, believe me," said Smiler stoutly.

"Where do you work, then? Still at the garage, Heytesbury way?"

"Not now. Got a job at Danebury House. With Mrs. Lakey."

"Oh, her. My dad knows her, too." She giggled. "Lash-'em-and-Bash-'em Lakey he calls her. Says she should have been a man. But he likes her."

"So do I," said Smiler. He grinned at the description of Mrs. Lakey. It was not far off the mark.

Then, with a sly twinkle in her eye, Pat said, "Still dye your hair, then?"

Under his tan Smiler blushed. "What do you mean?"

Pat laughed. "Girl I know in Woolworth's says you used to buy hair dye there – and sun-tan stuff."

Thinking quickly, Smiler said, "What if I did? It wasn't for me."

"For who, then?"

"Well. . . . For my Uncle Joe."

"What's he want it for?"

Desperate, feeling himself led into deep waters, Smiler said, "I can't really tell you. He mixes it all together and . . . and . . ." A brainwave came to him. "Well, if I tell you, promise never to let on to anyone? You'd get Uncle Joe in trouble."

"Promise."

"Well, this mixture. He uses it on white hens' eggs. Dyes 'em brown and it don't come off when you boil 'em. People prefers brown eggs and Uncle Joe sometimes only has white ones. But don't you tell."

Pat laughed. "What a crook. But I won't tell."

It took Smiler another ten minutes to get rid of her. He went back, with his trout, feeling limp with all the effort of making up his story, and had two mugs of cider instead of one with his dinner.

*　　*　　*

When the cheetah cubs were well over a month old they no longer stayed all day in the valley-side den. Although they were growing stronger each day, they were still clumsy on their feet and were a long way from being able to hunt for themselves. A rabbit or a hare could easily outrun them. Early each morning and late in the evening Yarra would take them out on to the hillside or up over the ridge on to the plain. For their education she would stalk and catch a mouse or shrew. Without killing the animal, she would release it so that the cubs would chase it. Then they would fight and quarrel as to which one should eat it.

Yarra never took them far away. She stayed by them during the day and made sure that they never went far beyond the entrance to the den. Sometimes when they were out together she would leave them briefly to hunt down a rabbit or a hare, and then, the cubs following, trot back to the den where they would all eat. Although her milk was now drying up, the two cubs still suckled at her during the night. Feeding the cubs during the day and keeping near them often left Yarra hungry. When they were fast asleep at night, and there was no danger of their straying, Yarra would go out on her own and kill for herself.

The nights now were mostly warm and light. Her eyesight was keen and it was seldom that she failed to turn up some game. She knew now the patches of bracken and small spinneys where the deer rested. She hunted always upwind, waiting for the scent of deer, hare or pheasant and partridge to come drifting down to her.

It was towards the end of May that Smiler first saw the cubs. Always when he was Imber way in the evenings he would take up a position on the far side of the valley and spend half an hour watching the entrance to the den. One evening he saw Yarra come out of the entrance and stand sniffing the air for a while. She moved farther out and the two cubs followed her.

Smiler nearly dropped his field glasses in surprise. Although he knew from local gossip that Yarra was a female, it had never occurred to him that she would have cubs. No mention had ever been made that she was carrying young when she had escaped.

Tense with excitement, he watched Yarra lead the cubs along the valley side. He saw her pouncing into the long grass after mice and grinned and chuckled to himself when the clumsy cubs imitated her example.

He went back to Joe that evening hardly able to conceal his excitement. He wanted to tell Joe all about it. In fact, he felt guilty that he couldn't share this wonderful piece of news with Joe, but he knew what Joe was like. It would make such a good story in the bar of the Angel Inn that Joe would never be able to keep it to himself.

So, Smiler kept quiet. It gave him a nice warm feeling that he was the only one who knew. It was his secret. Also, there was another feeling in him. Yarra had escaped from captivity. She had become a wild animal again and was raising a family. She was doing it, too, in a wild area of ground right in the heart of civilized England. Smiler, although town-bred, had now become a country boy. From talks with Joe and Mrs. Lakey and – most of all – with Miss Milly, he knew how the countryside was becoming spoiled and polluted and how hard it was these days for wild animals to survive. The hedgerows in which the birds nested were being pulled down and wire fences put in their place, making it harder for them to find breeding sites. He knew that mechanical reapers and binders had almost exterminated the corncrakes. He knew, too, that long ago Salisbury Plain had held the great bustard. He heard Miss Milly go on about the use of pesticides and chemical fertilizers that poisoned birds and animals and seeped into the rivers to kill fish. Sometimes he even felt bad about the poaching that he and Joe did, but as the game they took was usually rabbit, hare, pheasant or woodpigeon of which there were plenty he did not feel too guilty. That Yarra – not even a native animal – was managing to survive in the midst of all this gave him a great sympathy for her. He was determined that Samuel M. wasn't going to be the one to give her away.

*　　*　　*

Meanwhile other secrets were being kept or defended unknown to Smiler.

First of all there was Major Collingwood, who by now had discovered the loss of his old green anorak, and guessed, too, what had happened to the old bicycle. Weeks before, during his dinner with Mr. Coke, he had pretended that he wanted to be brought up to date on the local events which had occurred while he and Mrs. Collingwood had been abroad. He was told, of course, about the escaped cheetah, Yarra. He was told, also, a lot of other things which were of no great interest to him. But he *was* told that a young lad, named Samuel Miles, who had run away from a reform school only to be caught by the police, had escaped again in a storm while being taken to Salisbury. The escape had taken place some six or eight miles south of Warminster. This interested Major Collingwood very much. "Hunted's" letter, he felt, read like a young lad's letter.

Some days later, he went into the police station at Warminster. He knew the Police Inspector there and got a description of this Samuel Miles and all the facts that were known about him.

The Police Inspector, who was a friend of the Major, said, "What do you want to know all this for?"

The Major winked and said, "Sounds a very enterprising young chap – if *you* haven't picked him up yet. I thought I'd like to try my hand at it."

"Well – you'll have to go abroad again if you want him. He wrote a letter to his sister some months ago, saying he was shipping to sea."

By the time the Major left he had been given the address of Ethel and Albert. A few days later he drove to Bristol to see them. Of course, he knew by now that Samuel Miles was very fair-haired and very freckled. The question of hair dye and sun-tan stain no longer puzzled him.

When he met Ethel and Albert and talked to them there was no doubt in his mind that the person who had taken his bicycle and anorak, eaten his wife's sardines, borrowed his sixpenny pieces (and paid them back) and stained the bathroom curtain was none other than Samuel Miles, known as – Albert told him this – Smiler. Ethel, who had got it back from the police, showed him the letter which she had received from Smiler. One glance told the Major that the handwriting was the same.

The Major said, "Do you think he really went to sea?"

Albert said, "Could have done. It's in the blood. That's where his Dad is – and won't be back for another six months or more."

"There's more than the sea in his blood," said Ethel. "There's wildness. Bad company did it. Led 'im astray. Fancy – knocking an old lady down and taking her bag."

"I don't believe it!" said Albert.

"You did when it happened," said Ethel.

"Changed my mind," said Albert. "Smiler wouldn't 'ave done that. And wherever he is, Smiler won't turn up until his Dad's back. Thinks the world of him, he does. Thinks he can straighten it out. You mark my words – moment his Dad's back, he'll turn up."

"You must both be very worried about him," said the Major.

Albert grinned. "About Smiler? No. If ever

there was a boy that could look after himself, it's Smiler."

When the Major left he was inclined to agree. He found himself more than ever interested in Smiler. Driving home Major Collingwood decided that if Smiler had used the cottage and the barn then someone around the place, one of his friends or Mr. and Mrs. Bagnall, or their daughter might have seen him. He decided to make a few innocent enquiries. He asked Mr. Bagnall and got no help from him. He asked Mrs. Bagnall with the same result. Then one day, meeting Pat Bagnall pushing her bicycle up the hill from the bridge, he stopped and had a chat with her. He talked about this and that for a while and then said, "While I was away did you ever see a young lad – say between fifteen and sixteen – around the place? Tallish, strong lad, he'd be. Darkish brown hair and very sun-tanned. He could have been wearing a pretty old, green anorak."

Pat thought for a moment, but not because she didn't know the answer. It was an exact description of Johnny Pickering. She knew the Major well. He was a nice man and she liked him. But she liked Johnny, too. The Major's innocent question did not fool her. He had asked it in just the same way as her mother and father did when they were trying to get something out of her, or to trick her into giving something away she didn't want to give. So she said casually, "No, sir, I can't say that I did."

And that – for all his cleverness and professional training – was as far as Major Collingwood got for the moment.

*　　*　　*

It was about this time that Mrs. Lakey discovered that the Boy was living with Joe.

Mrs. Lakey was a keen fisherwoman. On two mornings while fishing the pool below the hatchway for trout she had looked across the field and seen Johnny feeding the pigs in Joe's ramshackle pen. As, on each occasion, the time was half-past seven of a Sunday morning – for Mrs. Lakey believed that it was the early fly-fisher who caught the best trout – she found it a little unusual.

A few days later when she had to call on Joe to give him some directions about dogs' meat supplies she tackled him in her usual straightforward manner.

"Joe," she said.

"Yes, Ma'am?"

"Is that Boy living with you?"

"What boy, Ma'am?"

"Don't wriggle like a worm on a hook with me, Joe. The Boy."

"Oh, you mean Johnny, Ma'am."

"You know perfectly well who I mean. He's living with you?"

"Yes, Ma'am."

"Why?"

"Well, 'cos in a way, I'm kind of his uncle. Distantly relationed, you might say, to his aunt."

"Being you, you might say anything. Why isn't he with his aunt?"

"The one at Crockerton, you mean, Ma'am?"

"I've never heard of another."

Joe smiled. "Oh, yes, Ma'am, he's got another. What lives in Bristol. And that's where 'is Crockerton auntie is right now. Lookin' after her, 'cos she's sick. Got a very bad leg. Plays her up somethin'

cruel every summer. Not to mention hay fever.
Martyr she is to every ache and pain goin'. I remember 'er as a small girl – always a-pickin' up
somethin' or the other. A medical wonder she is,
really. Once 'ad mumps three times running as a
girl –"

"I don't imagine she could have had it as a boy.
And I'm not in the mood for medical fairy stories.
The Boy lives here with you?"

"Yes, Ma'am."

"With his aunt's permission because she's away?"

"Yes, Ma'am."

"And you're kind of distantly his uncle?"

"Yes, Ma'am."

"And no doubt you're seeing he doesn't get into
bad ways?"

"Yes, Ma'am."

"Never poaches, does he?"

"Oh, no, Ma'am."

"Or worms for trout?"

"Oh, no, Ma'am. And he goes to church sometimes of a Sunday." Joe put on a very serious face.
"And I really do hope, Ma'am, as how you don't
think that I ain't a fit and proper person to bring
up me own nephew. Ain't he given you every
satisfaction at Danebury, Ma'am?"

"He has, Joe. And that's the way I want it to go
on. So, you watch your step with him. He's a good
boy as boys go."

"The best, Ma'am. Couldn't be in better hands
than with me, Ma'am. Though I says it meself."

"And if you didn't say it yourself who else would?"

When Mrs. Lakey got back to Danebury House
she told Miss Milly about the Boy's change of abode.

Mrs. Lakey privately felt that Joe was as fit a person as anyone for a boy to live with, though she wouldn't have said so to his face. If fishing was dull she wasn't above putting a worm on a hook herself to get a trout. Apart from all this, Mrs. Lakey was a person who – though always ready to help if asked – was a great believer in letting other people, especially young people, work out their own problems. She didn't know what the Boy's problem was, but as far as she could see he was coping with it perfectly capably at the moment.

11

∽ Two Mothers Meet ∽

By the first of June the cheetah cubs were seven weeks old. They were faster and steadier on their feet and could mouse-hunt for themselves, and were sometimes quick enough to take a slow-moving young lark or green plover in the long grasses. But they were still too young to run down a rabbit or a hare. Yarra provided the bulk of their food for them. The odd small stuff they caught for themselves would by no means have kept them alive.

However, there were times now when Yarra, sensing the future when they would have to fare for themselves, would sometimes cuff them away from the game she brought back. She was deliberately making them hungry now and then to strengthen their own hunting instincts. She would eat first, spitting and mock-snapping at them if they tried to approach until she had had her fill. If she awoke in the night to find them sucking at her dugs she would roll away from them, denying them the little milk flow that remained. Also in her, though not understood by her, was now a different kind of restlessness from the one she had known when she had been carrying her young. Yarra, like all her kind, was a sociable, pack animal. She did not like to live alone. Now that the cubs were growing and her maternal instinct had been satisfied, there was a new want in her. She had a need for the company of her own kind. This restlessness made her, when she left the cubs sleeping in the den, roam wider than she had done in the past. Somewhere in the vastness of the plain there had to be others of her kind, another Apollo to mate with, and other cheetahs to pack and hunt with. It was this that one night took her quartering and hunting into the face of a stiff north wind which was blowing almost a gale across the plain.

Once or twice she put up a rabbit, began the chase and then broke off. She was hungry but there was a stronger need inside her. Within an hour she was, although still on the plain, in new country to her. The wind whipped and flattened the tall grasses, blowing out of a cloudless sky that was ablaze with stars. Now and again she heard a small brown owl call. She watched the navigation lights of an airliner wink and blink across the sky. She scented deer twice but ignored the instinct to hunt.

Eventually she came out on to a high bluff at the northern extremity of the plain. A wire fence ran along the ridge of the bluff. Below, the land fell away into a great valley, the fields seeded with corn, the long slopes broken here and there with patches of woodland. Two miles away the occasional headlights of a car moved along an unseen road.

Yarra turned left along the fence, the wind buffeting at her thick, rough coat. Once she squatted on her haunches, sphinx-like and immobile, and then raised her head and gave two or three angry, rasping calls. She moved on and put up a rabbit from the lee of a gorse bush. She leapt and caught it by the neck, clamped her jaws hard, holding it until it died of suffocation. She dropped it and passed on.

When the fence angled downwards, following the slope of a combe-side, she followed it for a hundred yards to the foot of the combe. Here the fence ran along the edge of a large grove of tall beech trees. The high wind was bending and whipping the leafy top branches of the trees, making a loud soughing and whistling noise. Yarra stopped just short of the wood. Beyond the fence was a pasture field, the grass short from cattle grazing. A new scent came downwind to her.

It was a scent she had known before, but not for a long time now. Sometimes it had come to her in the cheetah enclosure at Longleat. She had also known it now and again in her first days of escape. She lifted her muzzle into the wind and took the scent. From the side of the wood which ran down the edge of the pasture there came a low, anxious, bleating sound. With the sound came a movement which Yarra saw at once.

At the woodside in the pasture something small and white stirred. The bleating sound came again, almost drowned by the rushing noise of the wind through the beeches.

The white object moved again but stayed in the same spot. Curious, Yarra leapt the fence and began to walk slowly towards the object.

The side of the beech wood bordering the field had been fenced off with strands of barbed wire which ran on thick posts. Posts and barbed wire were old and in places had collapsed. Twenty yards from Yarra strands of wire lay coiled and twisted on the ground. Caught by the leg in one of the coils was a small calf. In its struggles to escape the coil had pulled tighter and now it was firmly trapped. It was an Ayrshire calf, white-coated with a scattering of brown markings.

As Yarra approached it made an anxious, lowing sound and then stood still. It saw Yarra. Yarra watched the calf. It was no larger than some of the deer she hunted and she waited for it to move. From its scent she knew it was good eating. The fact that it stood still made her curious. Slowly, with her high-shouldered, deliberate walk, she paced towards the calf, but made a small half-circle to come past it. This brought her slightly upwind of the calf and her scent reached it. Catching Yarra's scent, and instinctively sensing the menace in the way the cheetah walked, the calf plunged and bleated and tugged against the wire that was trapping one of its hind legs. The length of wire pulled away from a holding staple in its rotting post. The calf bounded forward about six feet and was brought up with a jerk as the wire was held by the staple fastening in the next post.

The movement excited Yarra and she raced in and leapt. She landed on the calf's back and brought it crashing to the ground. Yarra's jaws clamped across the back of the calf's neck, choking all sound from the animal.

Her weight holding the calf down, Yarra tightened her grip. The calf kicked and struggled under her as she slowly throttled it, worrying and shaking its neck. High above, the wind, funnelling up the narrow combe, roared and whistled through the tall beeches, ripping off leaves and small twigs.

From farther down the sloping pasture the calf's mother had heard the distress calls of its young. She came downwind now, along the edge of the wood, seeking her calf. The wind carried her scent to Yarra, but her nostrils were full of the same scent from the calf. Also, Yarra heard no sound of the cow's movement towards her because it was drowned by the high soughing of the gale wind blowing through the trees.

The calf died under Yarra. She opened her jaws and released it. As she did so, she saw the movement of the Ayrshire cow almost on top of her.

The Ayrshire was a big animal. She had calved more than once before. She had a sleek white hide, blotched with cherry-red and brown markings over her forequarters. Like all Ayrshires her horns were very distinctive. They were long, and curved outwards and upwards and then slightly backwards. Formidable weapons. Under any other circumstances the cow would never have approached Yarra. But now she was impelled by her maternal instincts.

She lowered her head and rushed at Yarra. Yarra turned and leapt sideways to avoid her. She was a fraction too late. As she rose into the air, the cow jerked her head with a quick sideways slash of her horns. The left-hand, long, curving horn struck Yarra in the side, daggering deep into her belly just below the bottom of her rib cage.

Yarra gave a sharp angry, spitting snarl of rage and pain as she was flung high through the air. She thudded to the ground, rolled over, found her feet and then raced away as the cow came charging after her.

Yarra leapt the boundary fence and kept moving fast. Blood dripped from her wound. She went up to the head of the combe and headed southwards, back across the plain towards her den and her cubs.

171

As she moved, the pain in her belly nagged her. Once she halted and sat and licked at the wound.

Behind her in the pasture field the Ayrshire cow nuzzled and sniffed at the prostrate form of the calf. No movement came from it. (The next morning when the farmer saw it, he was to think that foxes had found the trapped calf and killed it, but had been driven off by the mother before they could eat it.)

Yarra took a line straight across the plain for her den and her cubs. She had three miles to go. With every step she took her pain increased and she grew more and more exhausted, and weaker and weaker. Behind her the gale-flattened grasses and the bare tracks were spotted with the trail of her life blood.

She kept on, following her line and her instinct to return to her cubs. Now and again she stumbled, only to pick herself up and move on. She reached the top of the ridge above the den and half-rolled, half-slid down the slope to the little screen of trees in front of the cave entrance.

She stood at the entrance, exhausted, her flanks heaving with the effort of breathing, her head dropping lower and lower on her long neck. She took a step forward to the entrance, staggered and fell. As she struggled to rise again and reach her cubs, she died.

*　　*　　*

Yarra died on a Friday long before daybreak. As morning came the wind which had been all night in the north slewed round into the north-west and brought thick, low-flying clouds sweeping over the plain. Rain began to fall steadily, a hard, warm, persistent summer rain.

The cubs, waking from sleep at first light, came out of the den and found their mother. She lay stretched out stiffly, the rain soaking into her pelt. They sniffed around her, not understanding her immobility. The male pawed for a moment or two at her neck to wake her and butted at her with his head. Then, not liking the hard, driving rain, he shook his body free of the clinging water drops and trotted slowly back into the den. The female stayed outside longer. She was hungrier than her brother. This was the time of day when normally Yarra took them for their morning hunting. She walked around Yarra making small mewing noises and then, getting no response, bad-tempered little spitting sounds. She crouched, flicked her small tail and jumped once or twice playfully at Yarra's flank. Yarra showed no movement. The cub, hungry, nuzzled at Yarra's dugs, hoping for milk. No milk came. After a while she moved back into the cave.

Yarra lay under the rain. The water, gathering on the steep slope above the den, now began to run down through the grasses in growing trickles and rivulets.

The mate of the carrion crow which Yarra had killed came flying low along the valley ridge. It saw Yarra and wheeled and circled for a while over her. Not trusting the immobility of the body below, it slid away down the valley to forage among the Imber village ruins.

The rain lasted all day. Down at Danebury House Smiler worked wearing an old Army groundsheet tied over his shoulders. Although he wanted the rain to finish, he knew that it could well last all day. It was coming on a strong wind out of the north-west, the kind of wind his father always called a *cat's nose* wind, though his father couldn't tell him why sailors gave it that name. He wanted the rain to finish before the evening came because he had planned to go up on the plain to see if he could spot Yarra and her cubs hunting.

At six o'clock as he cycled back to Joe's cottage, it was still raining. The river was beginning to rise fast, and the road ditches and drains gurgled and spouted with torrents of frothing brown water. Smiler realized that there was no hope that it would stop that evening. He decided that after his supper he would walk from the cottage to the main road and get the bus to Warminster. There was a good film showing which he wanted to see. With luck, he thought, he might persuade Joe to come and then they would go in the old green van and Joe would let him drive. Often now, Joe would let him take the wheel. Smiler was becoming a fairly confident driver, though Joe wouldn't let him drive in Warminster itself for fear of being caught by the police. Smiler wasn't yet old enough to have a provisional driver's licence. However, along the country roads Joe didn't mind a button about Smiler driving.

Up on the plain the rain had kept the cubs to the cave all day. Now and again one or other would venture out and inspect Yarra. As there was still no movement from her they eventually gave it up and huddled together at the back of the den, growing hungrier with each passing hour.

Towards midnight the rain stopped. The sky cleared swiftly of clouds and the fresh-washed stars shone down diamond-bright. The male cub, aware of the absence of rain noises in a moment of wakefulness, got up, stretched himself, and moved towards the mouth of the den. He was hungry. The lashing rain which he disliked had gone, and he knew that on the valley slope there were mice and shrews and small roosting birds to be caught.

He was two feet from the mouth of the cave when there was a noisy, rumbling sound. The few stars on the low horizon which he could see beyond the cave entrance suddenly disappeared. Something large and heavy hit him sharply across the neck. He spat and snarled with anger and bounded back to the rear wall of the den – as the roof of the cave entrance collapsed.

Weakened and loosened by the persistent rain which had soaked all day into the ground, the ancient archway of the tunnel entrance had suddenly subsided and sealed up the entry to the den.

Outside, the ground above the cave slipped forward in a minor avalanche, sweeping turf and chalk and stones downwards in a spreading fan which half-buried Yarra's body. When the movement ended all that could be seen of Yarra was her head and shoulders and her forelegs. Behind her the mouth of the cave was blocked. Inside against the rear wall, the two cubs huddled together in fright.

Later that night a travelling fox caught Yarra's scent and came a little way down the valley side to investigate. It sat for a long time looking at Yarra and then moved on. At first light the two buzzards, spiralling hundreds of feet above, saw her. The sandmartins hawking the early morning midges and gnats low along the hillside saw her. A white-bellied mouse rummaging among the branches of the tree-screen saw her. All of them knew her and all of them still kept their distance.

In the cave behind her the two cubs mewed, growled and spat, knowing only their hunger and growing thirst. The male cub explored the blockage and found a small puddle of water trapped in a hollow of the tunnel floor. He lapped at it and was joined by the other cub. By mid-morning their water supply had been exhausted.

At noon Smiler, who had planned to go up on the plain as soon as he was free, was asked by Miss Milly if he would mind staying and working through the Saturday afternoon. She and her sister were going to Salisbury, and two different lots of people were coming to Danebury Kennels to collect their dogs.

Mrs. Lakey and Miss Milly did not return until six o'clock, but when Smiler got back to Joe's cottage, knowing he still had plenty of time to go up on the plain for a few hours, Joe said:

"You thinking of going up top for a few hours tonight, Johnny?"

"Well, I was, Joe, if it's all right."

Joe shook his head. "It's just the opposite. All left. Heard in the Angel this lunch time that the Army people is 'avin' a special all-night exercise up there. They'll be goin' in about now and won't be out until mid-day tomorrow. Thought I'd tip you off."

"But they wouldn't see me, Joe."

"Too risky, me lad. They might be up to anything tonight. Place jumpin' with troops – and helicopters, flares and Old Nick knows what up in the sky. You keep out of there until tomorrow mid-day."

"But Joe, I'd be –"

"Nothing doing, Johnny. I got a responsibility for you. Seein' that you live 'ere and, in a way, I'm sort of your uncle. No, you want to go anywheres tonight then go down to the river. This rain'll 'ave made the big trout lively and fast on the fin."

So Smiler – although he had an inward tussle with himself – went down to the river and contented himself with a brace of nice trout.

Up on the plain during the night the cubs moved restlessly and hungrily in their den, feeling the rumble through the earth of tanks passing up the valley below. They heard, too, the thudding vibrations of exercising troops moving along the ridgeway and the muted gnat-sound of helicopters that passed low over the plain. Now and again, too, came the far thumps of shells falling and exploding.

*　　*　　*

Just before twelve the next day, Smiler cycled up to the Heytesbury Vedette hut, going fast past the entrance of Danebury House in case Tonks should be about and spot him. If the Vedette hut were un-manned and the red danger flag not flying he knew that there would be no troops about. He carried his lunch and his field glasses in a haversack on his back, and he was wearing the Major's old green anorak.

The hut was empty and no flag flew. He hid his bicycle in a field down the road. In a few minutes he was heading across the plain by one of his many routes to Imber. He had no fear of Land Wardens because they never showed in their Land-Rovers an hour or so either side of mid-day on a Sunday.

He came down the valley slope past the old church

into Imber. He crossed the road and circled away behind the ruined Imber Court and up the far valley side to his favourite spot for watching Yarra and the den.

It was a clear warm day. He settled himself in his grassy hollow and took out his field glasses and polished the lens and eye-pieces.

The moment he focussed on the mouth of the den he saw the half-buried Yarra. At first he thought she was just sunning herself against the cave mouth. Then he saw the scar on the slope above the cave. The glasses brought up clearly the torn turf and the bare soil and the piled debris closing the mouth of the cave. For a moment he sat there too surprised to know what to do or think. He looked at Yarra again and this time realized with a sharp pang of anguish that she *really was* half-buried.

He jumped to his feet and avoiding all cover began to run down the valley side. However, at the bottom of the valley he stopped. His heart was bumping and he was panting for breath but, over his shock and distress at the thought of Yarra being dead, good sense was suddenly taking control. Yarra *might not* be dead. She might just be trapped and unconscious. If she were still alive she could be dangerous. You've got to go cautious, Samuel M., he told himself. And what about the cubs? Where were they?

He went up the valley side at an angle that would hide him from the road through Imber and also take him clear of the cave. Reaching the ridgetop, he went over it and moved slowly back along it until he judged that he was level with the cave.

He crawled through the grass. Long ago he had

learnt not to expose himself on any skyline of the plain if he could help it. He peered over the side of the steep drop and had a clear view of Yarra. From the way she lay he was certain she was dead. Her pelt was matted and dirty from the past rain and earthfalls. Her head was twisted a little upwards and her mouth gaped unnaturally, showing her teeth. As Smiler saw this there was a dead weight inside him of sadness. Hard against the back of his eyes he felt the sting of tears and fought them back. He and Yarra had, in a way, escaped together. Now, Yarra was gone. It was awful. It ought not to have happened. She should be still as he was, free and fending for herself.

Lying there, he buried his face in his arms for a while. Then he slowly got up and went to the little plateau where Yarra lay behind the screen of trees and bushes. There was absolutely no doubt in his mind now that she was dead. Even so, he approached her warily. Leave nothing to chance, his dad had always said. Better be safe than sorry.

But there was no doubt about it. Yarra was gone. He moved to her and put a hand on her neck. It was stiff and there was no warmth in the pelt. He looked round and saw the blocked mouth of the cave and guessed how the collapse had happened . . . during all that recent rain.

Then, as he looked at the jumbled pile of loose turf and soil, he heard very faintly a thin half-mewing, half-complaining noise. He went to the blockage and put his ear against it. The noise came again. This time, mixed with the mewing, was a brief, angry, spitting sound. Although he didn't know it, it came from the male cub.

Smiler sat back on his hunkers and scratched his head. For the moment Yarra was gone from his mind. The cubs were trapped inside the cave. What on earth was he to do?

Now Smiler was nothing if not practical and resourceful. Faced with a big problem he knew how to worry his way through it and sort out the right decisions to be made. And he had a big problem – and a lot of little ones – on his hands right now.

Take it slowly, Samuel M., he told himself. Sounds as though the cubs are both still alive. Thing Number One is, you've got to get them out. Thing Number Two is. . . . He began to sort his way through the situation.

As he sat there the buzzards up above saw him and swung away. All day they had watched Yarra and had been on the point of closing in for a cautious inspection. The carrion crow in a tall treetop at the valley mouth could see him. The carrion crow had become bolder during the day and had twice walked around Yarra from a safe distance but had lacked the courage to move in close. The sandmartins hunting the high-flying noon insects above him, and a hare couched farther down the valley side, had long seen him. Dozens of birds and animals were well aware of Smiler as he sat on his hunkers dealing with his problem.

A few minutes later and Smiler was making his way over the ridgetop. Not far away was one of the many firepoints which were dotted across the plain. These held beating poles for fighting the rapid fires often caused by some soldier throwing away a burning cigarette end. The one he was heading for, he knew, held an old spade.

The cubs had to be dug out. They would be hungry, thirsty, and frightened – and young animals in that state might be difficult to handle. He would have to face that one. Neither of them was big enough to do him any real harm so long as he watched himself. Then there was Yarra. He had to do something about her.

The next three hours were very busy ones for Smiler. He had to go down twice to Imber, and each time he had to keep a sharp watch for any patrolling Land Warden. In those three hours there was a time of great joy for Smiler and a time of great sorrow.

12

∽ *Smiler Takes Charge* ∽

Within twenty minutes Smiler was back with the spade. He began to dig at the blocked entrance to the cave, working hard and fast and expertly. Fortunately the collapsed roof of the den opening was all loose soil and turf. There were no heavy stones amongst the debris. After about ten minutes hard going he had worked his way through the top part of the blockage, digging slightly downwards all the time. Suddenly his spade went through the last of the block. A small hole about the size of a man's head opened up and the sunlight poured through it.

He stopped digging and waited, listening. Inside the cave, the two cubs had long heard the sound of Smiler working away with the spade. When he finally broke through both of them were huddled together against the back wall of the den. The sudden sunlight blinded them. The male cub arched his back and snap-hissed, half in fear and half in defiance. The female crouched by him, more hungry than frightened, and gave a series of small mews.

Outside, Smiler clicked his tongue and gave a few low encouraging cries. He reached back and got his haversack. Inside, wrapped in grease paper for his lunch, was a small, cold, roast chicken. He broke off one of the legs and held it just outside the hole.

He couldn't see the cubs, but he could hear them moving and crying now.

Inside the cave both cubs suddenly got the scent of the chicken. They ceased their noise. The male cub, drawn first by the smell of food, moved slowly forward towards the patch of daylight at the front of the cave. Two feet from it he stopped. He could see part of Smiler's face and the smell of the chicken was now stronger. The hunger in him overcame his fear. He climbed up over the loose soil to the opening.

Smiler, shaking with excitement, saw the male cub's head framed just inside the opening, saw the short stubby ears, the black lines of the face masking and the orange-brown pelt, black-spotted, of the cub's neck. Behind the male cub, the face of the female cub appeared. Smiler reached forward and dropped the chicken leg just inside the opening. The movement made both cubs jump back a little, spitting and hissing. Smiler, holding himself very still, guessing that movement would alarm them, made soft encouraging noises.

After a moment or two the male cub came forward slowly, then suddenly pounced, grabbed the chicken leg, and disappeared back into the cave, followed by the female cub. Smiler was overcome with a great joy. Frightened they might be, but they had taken food from him.

He tore the chicken in two and threw half of it well into the cave. It landed near the female cub who was worrying around her brother to get at the leg which he was eating and guarding from her with swift strokes of his forepaws. She turned and seized it and ran into a corner of the den. As she did so, the sunlight funnelling into the cave was abruptly blocked off. Undisturbed by this the two went on with their eating.

Outside Smiler had blocked the little opening he had made by piling large turfs and clods of earth into it. It was all part of the plan he had worked out when he had faced the problem on his hands. The cubs had to be fed and watered, but for the time being he could not risk their coming out of the den and escaping from him. Yarra was dead now. They were *his* cubs and he had to look after them sensibly and see that they came to no harm until he could work out a plan for them.

While the cubs ate in darkness, Smiler dragged Yarra free from the soil and turf that partly covered her. He knew exactly what he must do with her. Not that he liked the idea, but it seemed the only thing for him to do. If he buried her on the hillside or up on the plain he could never cover up the evidence of his digging. Some soldier might spot it, or scavenging rats or foxes might find it.

Scattered all over the plain were dozens of old wells which had been dug in the years long past when the land had not belonged to the army, and the long plain sweeps were grazed or tilled. Smiler knew such a well at the head of the valley. Hating every moment, but knowing he had to do it, he dragged Yarra a quarter of a mile up the valley to the well. It was in a little clump of thorn trees. The Army authorities had years ago capped most of the wells with concrete tops or wooden platforms so that the exercising troops should not fall down them by accident. This well had a timber top. The thick planks were loose in places. Smiler pulled a couple aside. The well was a very deep one. He dragged Yarra across the platform and let her drop through the gap he had made. As he put the heavy planks back there were now tears in his eyes. It was a moment of great sorrow.

Keeping in cover all the way, he went back to Imber village and found an old bucket which he filled with water from the spring near Imber Court. He took the bucket back to the den, left it outside, and then went back again to the village. This time he returned with three or four short lengths of plank from the broken-up floor boards of one of the cottages, and a small, battered old tin bowl.

For the next hour Smiler worked away, keeping a sharp look-out for the movement of any Land Warden. He was following the plan he had worked out.

He opened up the small entrance to the cave, made it larger, and then tossed the last half of the chicken through to the cubs. They took it and began to quarrel over it. He filled the tin basin and put that through the opening on to the floor just inside. The smell of the water brought the cubs at once to the basin. To Smiler's delight, both cubs rushed to it and began to lap thirstily, taking no notice of him. He was tempted to reach his hand through and stroke them. He decided not to do this. He was country-wise enough now to know that if you wanted to be friends with an animal you never rushed things.

While the cubs drank and then went back to their chicken, Smiler worked at making a small plank doorway for the considerably reduced mouth of the cave. He arranged it so that he had three short planks fixed vertically down across the mouth. The middle plank he organized so that he could pull it upwards at will to make an opening. The outside planks he fixed firmly top and bottom with a packing of soil and turf which he firmed down with heavy strokes of the flat spade head.

When this was done Smiler tidied up the outside of the cave as well as he could, clearing the small plateau where Yarra used to sun herself. He spread turves and old leaf mould from under the tree screen around the place to make it look less disturbed. Then, knowing that the cubs were well fed and watered for the time being, he left them.

All the way back to Joe's cottage, while he went his secret ways across the plain with the larks giving their evening chorus above him, Smiler was occupying himself with *his real problem*.

Yarra was dead and the cubs were alive. But the cubs were not old enough to look after themselves. He ought to tell someone that they were up on the plain so that they could be caught and taken back, say, to Longleat where they would be looked after properly. But if he told Joe about them, or Miss Milly or Mrs. Lakey, it would mean that a lot of public attention would be drawn to himself. Publicity would lead him back to the reform school. He could, of course, just make an anonymous telephone call to the police or one of the Land Wardens, telling about the cubs but not giving his name. But not even that would save him, because the news would become public, be in all the papers and be talked about – and then Joe would hear about it. And Joe was clever enough to put two and two together. Joe liked having secrets and could keep them. Smiler suspected, however, that Joe couldn't keep a really big secret. Not when he had been an hour or two in the Angel. "Cheetah cubs up in a little old cave in Imber valley?" Joe would say to himself. "And some unknown person – sounded like a boy's voice it's said – telephoned about 'em. . . ?"

Joe would look at him, Smiler, across the supper table and say, "Wouldn't 'ave been you by any chance, would it, Johnny lad?" And that would be it. Joe had shown him all the secret ways around Imber and that part of the country. Joe knew how much time he spent up there. Joe would know that if *anyone* was ever going to spot Yarra's cave, and then find out she had cubs, and go to the trouble of digging them out and building a door. . . . Oh, Crikeys, thought Smiler. Joe would have it out of him in no time. And then the word would go round! He was pretty sure that Joe already didn't believe the story about his aunt at Crockerton. . . . Oh, Lordy. . . . There would be that reform school waiting. Once Joe knew something was bound to go wrong.

So, that evening, sitting by himself in the gloaming on the river bank – Joe was already away to the Angel – Smiler came to a big decision.

He *had* to keep free until his father returned. Also, he had to see that the cubs were properly looked after. That meant he had to telephone the police or some-one. And *that* meant that the moment he did so he would have to take off. Right away from this part of the world, covering his tracks as he went. He would have to go right away and find another job some-where. But he didn't want to move on. He liked working at Danebury House. He liked Miss Milly and Mrs. Lakey (though not quite so much), and he liked Joe (better than anyone), and, in a way, he quite liked seeing Pat Bagnall now and then and having a chat with her.

But, Samuel M., he told himself, no matter what *you* like and what *you* want to do – you've got to tell about the cubs. Samuel M., that means you *have got* to move on. Not today. Not tomorrow. But pretty soon. As soon as you've got a plan made out for yourself.

Sadly, Smiler went back to the cottage and counted his savings. He had thirty odd pounds, a few bits of clothing, a bicycle and a suitcase which he'd bought to carry his gear in. All he needed now, was a plan. It would have to be good, because when he disappeared *that* would start questions, too. . . . Crikeys, it wasn't going to be easy to work out.

* * *

However, during the next week while Smiler was worrying at his plan for disappearing, he had the cubs to look after.

This was very hard work. He was up before dawn and away from the cottage long before Joe was awake. He would ride up past Danebury House, hide his bicycle, and make his way across the plain to the cubs. Food was no problem. He packed his haversack with dog meat from Joe's store and dropped a shilling into Joe's cash box now and then to pay for it. He would give the cubs their breakfast, refill their water bowl, and then shut them up and be back at Danebury in time for work. In the evening when he had finished work at Danebury, he would take some dog meat from the kennel store and go back up to the cubs and give them their evening meal.

Within three days the cubs got to know him. When he came to the cave door he would whistle to them. The moment he pulled up the plank they would be waiting for him, snapping and spitting with excitement. But he was worried about giving them exercise. Young animals could not be kept shut up all the time. Fortunately the male cub solved this problem for him.

Smiler arrived on the fourth evening to find that the middle door plank had been butted away. Both cubs were playing around by the tree screen. He saw them as he came up the steep slope and they saw him.

Smiler stood where he was, not knowing what to do. Then, to his surprise, the cubs began to move down towards him. He gave his low whistle. They broke into a fast trot through the long grasses, every high-shouldered movement and graceful stride they made reminding him of Yarra.

Smiler crouched down. The cubs came to him, but stopped a few feet short. The female squatted on her haunches. The male circled slowly round at a safe distance. Smiler pulled his haversack round and took out a piece of meat and held it up. Immediately the female came towards him.

Smiler got to his feet and, holding the piece of meat high, began to move up to the den entrance. Both clubs followed him. Just before they reached the small plateau, the male cub made a sudden leap towards the meat that nearly took Smiler by surprise. It was a higher jump than he had thought the cub could make.

After that it was easy. Smiler tossed two large lumps of meat into the den and the cubs went in after them. Smiler watered them. Before he left, he made the door much firmer so that they could not get out. On the way back to the cottage he thought about exercising the cubs and worked out a plan for the next morning.

It worked perfectly. He pulled up the plank door and held his meat-filled haversack close to the opening. Both cubs came to it. Smiler moved away and slung his haversack high on his back. He moved up the valley side for a hundred yards. The cubs followed him and the scent of the meat in the haversack. When he turned and went back to the cave the cubs turned with him. At the cave entrance, he threw meat inside and the cubs went in after it. That was the beginning of their training, and they learnt quickly.

By the week-end, so long as he had meat in his haversack and they had not been fed, they would follow him. By the middle of the next week Smiler could hang his haversack high on a branch of one of the screening trees and walk off. The cubs would go with him, though the first time the male sat obstinately under the tree for a while.

At the end of two weeks, the rule was firmly fixed. Both cubs followed him for a walk before returning to the cave to be fed from the haversack that hung from the tree. By this time, too, the cubs would let him handle them, stroke them, and massage their necks which they loved. If they strayed a little from him they would come back at the sound of his whistle. Smiler was delighted with all this.

It was nearing high summer now. The cubs were

growing fast and were well used to Smiler. So long as the weather was good and the cubs were fed and watered, there was no hurry, Smiler told himself, about settling their future. The days wore into July and every morning and evening Smiler would exercise the cubs up the long narrow valley and across a small stretch of plain at its head. Fed or not, they came with him, answered his call, and had no fear of his touch. Though Smiler was always careful when he did this. Twice the male cub had scratched him inadvertently in a moment of rough play.

The buzzards knew the trio and so did the other birds and beasts. At the valley head one evening a young rabbit got up from the grass and the male cub went after it and caught it. For a moment or two Smiler did not know what to do. He realized that it would be dangerous to try and take the rabbit from the cub. So he turned and began to walk back towards the den. The female followed him. He whistled to the male as he walked. After a moment or two the male, mouth closed over the rabbit's neck, turned and followed him, carrying his prey. The male cub carried the rabbit back and into the den.

So, slowly, Smiler learnt how to handle the cubs in different situations and the cubs came to know Smiler. And Smiler gave them names. The male he called Rico and the female Afra. He didn't know why he called them that, but he was rather pleased with his inventions.

*   *   *

Although by now Smiler had long made up his mind

what he eventually must do about things he kept on putting it off because he enjoyed being with the cubs so much. Each time that he made up his mind to do something, he had changed it within a few minutes of being back with them.

During the fourth week of his taking charge of the cubs, unknown to him, a decision began to be made for him.

One Friday evening Joe said to him, "Johnny my lad, tomorrow afternoon I'm a-going to give you a treat. And don't tell me you don't want to come because you want to go up on that old plain. What you got hidden up there, anyways? A gold mine?"

"I just like being up there, Joe."

"And so do I, Johnny. But a change won't do you any harm. A treat I'm going to give you and a treat you're goin' to have. We'll be back by six so you can slip up there for an hour after, if you want."

So Smiler, who never liked disappointing Joe – and even felt a bit guilty for keeping his cheetah secret from him – said he would like to have a treat.

Joe duly gave him his treat, the both of them driving off in the green van. By the time Smiler – who had thoroughly enjoyed himself – got back he knew exactly how to solve part of his remaining problem.

While Joe was giving Johnny his treat, Major Collingwood was having tea with his wife at Ford Cottage. They were having it out on the small front lawn that overlooked the river. The Major, although he still thought about it now and then, had long ago lost his interest in tracing Mr. Hunted. He had come to a dead end. The Major was the kind of man, who when he came to a dead end, didn't like to stay there long. He turned round and found something else of interest to do.

He was reading his newspaper and feeling rather sleepy from the hot sun. The sound of the river running by lulled him. Now and again he dozed off as his wife chatted to him. Sometimes he came out of his doze to catch the end of one of her sentences and to make some polite reply.

From a somewhat deeper doze-off, he surfaced briefly to hear his wife finishing a sentence.

". . . and although they work him hard enough over there, I thought now in the long evenings he could give you a hand."

"Give me a what, dear?" The Major blinked his eyes open.

"Give you a hand in the garden. He's a good worker, Angela Lakey tells me."

A little more awake, the Major said, "Who is?"

Mrs. Collingwood laughed. "Why, Johnny, of course."

"Who on earth is Johnny?" asked the Major.

His wife shook her head. "Sometimes I think your memory is going altogether. Johnny, the boy who works for Danebury House. And if you want to know where Danebury House is, it's where I go riding sometimes as you well know. I've spoken to you about him before."

"Not that I remember. Perhaps I was asleep at the time."

"Well, he's a nice boy. He lives with that awful Joe Ringer. He's a tall, strong boy with dark-brown hair and sort of freckled under his sunburn. I don't know where Angela found him. She doesn't seem keen ever to talk about him. Almost as though

there was some sort of mystery about him, I feel."
She laughed. "You'd think he was an escaped
convict, or something. Would you like some more
tea, dear?"

The Major sat forward in his chair, suddenly
deep in thought. "Tea?" he questioned.

"Yes, dear. The brown liquid that comes out of a
teapot and which you drink from a teacup. Really,
I think this sun is too much for you!"

But it was not the sun that was too much for the
Major. It was his old interest in Mr. Hunted which
had suddenly revived, though he was careful not to
show it.

He said casually, "Oh, yes, I think I've seen him
cycling about Heytesbury. Does he wear an old
green anorak sometimes? Like one I used to have?"

"I believe he does. Yes, he does sometimes. Well,
anyway, I was thinking that if he had the time we
might . . ."

The Major didn't hear her because he was
thinking, too; thinking that he would like to have a
look at this Johnny, a good look without Johnny
seeing him.

This he managed to do twice during the next
few days. He also met Miss Milly in Warminster
shopping the following Monday and had a chat
with her – among other things about Johnny. He
learnt that Johnny had an aunt called Mrs. Brown
who lived at Hillside Bungalow in Crockerton. She
was away at the moment tending a sick sister in
Bristol. Since the Major lived almost in Crockerton
himself he knew perfectly well that there was no
Mrs. Brown and no Hillside Bungalow there. With
all this knowledge, his certainty grew that Johnny

was really Samuel Miles. The Major, who was a good-hearted, conscientious, and kind man, but one used to Army discipline, found himself with a problem which he knew would take him a little while to think out. To think out, that is, for the real good of Samuel Miles, known to his friends as Smiler or Johnny.

It was more than a week before the Major, who had a few other enquiries to make, came to his decision and knew exactly where his duty lay.

13

∽ The Sleep-walker ∽

Smiler was never to forget the happiness of his days
with Afra and Rico. They were bright summer days
and rainy summer days. They were days when the
movement of the cubs racing and hunting at the
top of the valley printed pictures in his mind which
he would always remember. They came to his
whistle now and, unless they were hunting, trotted
close to him. Their pelts were taking full colour,
the amber, black-spotted coats rippling above their
muscle movements. They caught mice and rabbits,
and twice they packed together and ran down a very
young hare. When they killed Smiler never attempted
to take their kill from them. If he had time he would
wait until they had eaten. Otherwise he would go
back to the den and they would follow, carrying
their catch. He still regularly fed and watered them.
Also, he had forever a watchful eye for Land Wardens
or late exercising troops.

Sometimes he lay in the grass and the cubs
would romp over him as they played together. The
early morning and late evening air was full of the
smell of wild thyme. With the passing of the days
Smiler hated the thought of the day that was coming,
the day already fixed in his mind when they would
have to part company. He would have liked to stay
up on the plain with them forever. If there had been
no other people to bother them they could have

lived easily. There was water, food to be found, and plenty of shelter. Even in the winter he reckoned they would be able to manage. He saw himself in a commodious cave, a fire burning at the entrance, and Afra and Rico lying together well away from the flames, while the winter wind shrieked outside. He knew it was all a dream. But it was a good dream to have.

One warm moonlit night, he spent the whole time on the plain with them because Joe had gone away on business to Southampton and was staying with a friend down there.

When Mrs. Lakey met him at the kitchen door next morning she took one look at him and said, "Boy, you're as red-eyed as an albino. Don't tell me you had too much of Joe Ringer's cider last night?"

"No, Mrs. Lakey, I'm always careful how much I have of that stuff."

"St. Patrick himself keep you that way, Boy. He always prescribed it in moderation – and left each mortal to decide for himself what moderation was."

At lunchtime Miss Milly said, "That's a bad scratch on your hand, Johnny. I'll fix it for you with a plaster."

Rico a little rough in play had bit lovingly at Smiler's hand that night and torn the flesh. While she was attending to his hand, Miss Milly went on, "Jelly and I are going to dinner with a Major Collingwood at Crockerton on Friday. He asked me some time ago if you'd care to do a little week-end gardening work for him? Shall I tell him, yes?"

Smiler's hair nearly stood on end.

He stammered, "Well . . . well, Miss Milly, I

don't think. . . . Well, I like to have a bit of time to myself at week-ends."

"And it's right you should. I'll tell him to cast his eyes elsewhere."

If he could have told her the truth Smiler would have said that the coming week-end was going to be his last at Danebury, his last in this part of the world. On Sunday morning he meant to be up early and away in Joe's green van with Afra and Rico. It would mean creeping into Joe's bedroom to get the key of the van from his jacket pocket, but Joe always slept like a log on Saturday nights after his visit to the Angel. Smiler knew that he would have no difficulty in getting the key. He planned to leave a letter for Joe explaining where he could find the van. The thought of leaving Joe was almost as bad as that of leaving the cubs.

The last few days of Smiler's time on the plain slid by. The buzzards had brought off a young one from a pair of eggs and were teaching it acrobatics high above. The carrion crow flew solitary about her foraging and scavenging. Charms of goldfinches worked the tall thistles and weeds on the plains, and the barn owls quartered silently and soft-winged on their night hunting. Each morning and evening Smiler was with Afra and Rico. He had put all his affairs in order ready to move off, to stay free until his father returned. He knew his father would believe him when he told him that he had not robbed the old lady. His father would turn the world upside down, too, until other people believed it – and then he wouldn't have to go back to the reform school. He hadn't robbed the old lady and that was that!

*　　*　　*

On Friday evening Mrs. Lakey and Miss Milly went to dinner with the Major and his wife. They had drinks in the evening sun on the lawn just outside the open dining-room windows. An occasional trout rose to a fly on the river, dimpling the surface. A kingfisher flashed downstream, and a family of yellow wagtails bobbed and played over the gravel spits along the banks.

Mrs. Lakey and Miss Milly were very old friends of the Major and his wife so that the Major did not much relish what he was going to have to say and do. Being a military man he had decided that, if a thing were to be done, then it was better to do it quickly.

Mrs. Lakey was seated with her glass of whisky, Miss Milly with her sweet marsala, Mrs. Collingwood with a glass of dry sherry, and the Major with a slightly larger whisky than the one he had given Mrs. Lakey because he felt he was going to need it.

After a few minutes pleasant social chat, the Major cleared his throat and said to Mrs. Lakey, "Angela, there's something which I must discuss with you and Milly. It's serious and it's about your boy, Johnny. Johnny Pickering who lives with Joe Ringer."

Miss Milly said, "Johnny's a good boy, Major. But he just wants his week-ends free. So I'm afraid he doesn't want to garden for you."

"Afraid of a little extra work. Like all boys," said Mrs. Lakey. "Though the Boy is better than most. Furlongs ahead of any other I know."

"No, I don't mean about working for me," said the Major.

199

"Then what else could you possibly mean, dear?" asked his wife. "After all, we can just get someone else to do –"

Very firmly, the Major said, "I am not talking about gardening. And I would appreciate it if you ladies would kindly give me your attention for a few minutes without interruption."

"Very military all of a sudden, isn't he, Jelly?" said Miss Milly. "Just like father used to be when anything went wrong. Like when one of the grooms –"

"Be quiet, Milly, and drink your marsala," said Mrs. Lakey. "Though how you can like the stuff –"

"What about Johnny, dear?" asked Mrs. Collingwood. "Has he been poaching with that awful Joe Ringer?"

Even more firmly, the Major said, "Dear ladies, I would like to get this matter settled, but if you keep interrupting it will take all night –"

"And the dinner will be spoiled," said Mrs. Lakey. "But carry on, Major. I think I know what maggot has got into your apple. The Boy is Samuel Miles, isn't he?"

The Major looked at her in astonishment, and cried, "You knew?"

"Almost from the first. You don't always have to look at a horse's mouth to tell its age. Think I can't spot it when a boy's got something to hide that dyed hair can't cover?"

"*Who* is this Samuel Miles?" asked Miss Milly.

"The Boy," said her sister.

"Your Johnny," declared the Major. "He's escaped from an approved school."

"Johnny's a good, kind, honest boy," said Miss

Milly stoutly. "I don't believe a word of anything you're going to say."

Mrs. Collingwood sighed. "So far as I am concerned I would just like to know what everyone is talking about."

"Then listen," declared the Major almost crossly. "His name is really Samuel Miles and he's been in this house, dyed his hair, and eaten our sardines, and taken my anorak and covered up his freckles and . . . How on earth, my dear, do you think your bathroom curtains were stained?"

Mrs. Lakey smiled and said, "It's the most lucid explanation I ever did hear, Major. Worthy of an Irishman. And what is more the Boy has no aunt called Mrs. Brown of Hillside Bungalow, Crockerton, and if he escaped from an approved school and then from the police, more power to his elbow. Any two things better escaped from I can't imagine. *But* it's not our job to do the work of approved schools or the police so –"

Pompously, the Major said, "He attacked an old lady and stole her handbag."

"Never!" said Miss Milly. "What an awful thing to say about Johnny! I think I must have some more marsala."

Mrs. Collingwood, moving to help Miss Milly to more marsala, said to her husband, "Darling, take a deep breath, count ten, and then start at the beginning. Funny, I thought it looked like your anorak. There was a splotch of red paint on it that –"

The Major snorted and cried, "Will you all listen to me!"

Mrs. Collingwood smiled, Miss Milly sipped at

her marsala and Mrs. Lakey began to light a small cheroot. A blackbird sang from an ash tree. In the woods across the river a woodpecker drummed against the trunk of a beech. A pack of sparrows began quarrelling on the thatched roof, and the Major – who had used almost his parade ground voice – began to explain, telling the story of Samuel Miles as he knew it.

One afternoon in Bristol an old lady had been jostled off the pavement by a boy and her handbag stolen. A policeman, seeing the act from a distance, had gone after the thief. Around the corner he had spotted a boy running down the pavement. The policeman had caught him and found that he was holding the old lady's handbag with ten pounds in it. The boy was Samuel Miles. His father was away at sea and he was living with a married sister. Samuel Miles had denied the theft, though he *had* been in some small bits of bother with the police before.

Samuel Miles' story, however, was that he had been standing just round the corner when a boy he knew had come rushing past him and had tossed him the handbag, shouting "Hide it!" The boy was one Johnny Pickering. They were not friends. In fact they disliked one another. Samuel Miles had said that when he was caught running away he was really running after Pickering to make him take the handbag back. Both boys were about the same height, and both had fair hair. Samuel Miles had said that Pickering must have seen the policeman and, once around the corner, tossed the handbag to him and run on.

But, the Major explained, in the juvenile court the father and the mother of Pickering had both sworn that their son had been at home all afternoon. One of their neighbours had sworn the same. The court had decided that Samuel Miles – and evidence had been given to show that Samuel Miles did not like Pickering – was lying to save himself. They had found him guilty and decided that he must go to an approved school.

At this point Miss Milly said stoutly, "It's not true. Johnny would never do such a thing."

"It's the father and mother of all lies," said Mrs. Lakey.

"I think, it's a lie, too," the Major agreed. "But the point is, if Johnny is to be proved innocent, it can never happen while he's on the run. We've got to tell the police about him. Then we can have the case re-opened. We can get at the truth and have him cleared. He's worked hard and honestly for you, Angela. He paid back what he borrowed from me – except the anorak and the old bike – and what do they matter? He's shown resource and initiative in looking after himself and –"

"I think, dear," said Mrs. Collingwood, "that we all understand and agree with you. But it does seem hard to go –"

"Snivelling to the police," said Mrs. Lakey. "It's like deliberately putting a good dog down before its time. But, there's some sense in what the Major says. How can the law do anything for the Boy unless the law has got the Boy?"

Miss Milly said, "You've known all this for a long time, Jelly. If you think he ought to be given up, why didn't you do it ages ago?"

"Because, Milly, I don't jump fences until I come to 'em. And this fence is now right under the horse's nose." She looked hard at Major Collingwood. "You believe in the Boy's innocence?"

"Absolutely. I made a few enquiries about this Pickering family. They haven't a good reputation. I think they were lying to protect their son."

"And you think you can clear things for the Boy?"

The Major said importantly, "Yes. I have friends in the police in Bristol. They'll listen to me. All we have to do is tell the police where Johnny is and then I'll lay a hundred to one we can clear things up."

"I don't like it," said Miss Milly. "You mean let them know *right away*? Think of poor Johnny at home now having his supper after a hard day's work and the police walking in and taking him to spend a night in a cell. . . . Oh, no!"

The Major pondered this, then he said deliberately, "You've a soft heart, Milly – but it's got to be done."

Miss Milly stood up. "You really want to ring up the police now?"

"Yes, Milly," said the Major.

"Then," said Miss Milly firmly, "don't expect me to sit down afterwards and take dinner in your house. How could I?" She turned to her sister. "Jelly, I'm going home. If anyone thinks I could take a bite of food knowing all the time that –"

"Milly," said Mrs. Lakey, "ease back in the saddle a bit." She turned to the Major, and went on, "The Boy has been free for months. Twelve hours' delay won't do any harm, and he's not going to run away because he knows nothing of all this –"

"And," interrupted Mrs. Collingwood, "I'm not having my dinner party ruined. We've got smoked salmon and then a beautiful piece of lamb, and a sweet it's taken me all afternoon to make. Milly and Angela are staying. You can tell the police first thing in the morning."

The Major looked at each woman in turn. After a few moments he shrugged his shoulders. "Well, I suppose it won't make any difference. All right. I'll telephone them first thing in the morning."

"And glad I am to hear it," said Mrs. Lakey, "for if Milly had gone, then so would I – and there's nothing I like better than smoked salmon and a nice piece of lamb."

"Poor Johnny," said Miss Milly. She sat down and took a sip of her marsala. "Never in my life will I believe that he ever robbed an old lady."

"We'll prove he didn't," said the Major. "But until it can be done, he's got to be held in custody by the proper authorities. That's the law."

"The law," said Miss Milly vigorously, "is an ass!"

"Agreed, Milly," said her sister.

At that moment Mrs. Bagnall, who helped Mrs. Collingwood when she gave a dinner party, appeared at the front door and said, "Dinner is served, madam."

*   *   *

While Mrs. Collingwood's dinner party was in progress, Smiler was walking back down the valley with Afra and Rico towards their den. The light was fast going from the western sky. The jackdaws were returning to their roosts in the church tower at Imber. Fox and badger were beginning their night prowls. Moths blundered through the warm, still air.

When they reached the entrance to the cave, Smiler knelt down and with either hand rubbed the rough-pelted necks of Afra and Rico. Afra purred and nuzzled her head against Smiler's bent knee. Rico turned and closed his jaws gently over Smiler's hand. He knew now just how hard he could hold without harming Smiler. In the pale light the golden eyes of the two animals shone softly, their black face-markings giving them a faint, laughing look.

Smiler was aware of a lump in his throat. Samuel M., he was telling himself, tomorrow night you'll be putting them away in the cave for the last time. Sunday morning, first thing, you'll be up and away with them. They won't see this old plain again, and neither will you. No, Samuel M., you won't see Danebury again, nor Joe, nor a lot of people and places you like. . . . Not for ages and ages, anyway. . . . Not until your old Dad comes back and can clear things up.

He stood up, tossed some meat into the cave and watched the cubs enter. Then he boarded up the entrance securely and began to make his way home.

When he reached Joe's cottage, it was nearly eleven o'clock. Joe was in the kitchen having a last glass of cider before going to bed. He offered Smiler some, but Smiler had a glass of milk instead.

"Been up top again then, Johnny?" asked Joe.

"For a bit."

Joe gave him a long look and said, "Milk ain't no good for what you got by the look of your face. For a bad case of the glooms there's nothin' like cider. Anything special happened?"

"No, I'm just tired, Joe," said Smiler.

"It's honest labour what does that. Been trying to avoid it all me life – without success. What about a bit of a singsong on the pianer then?"

"No, thanks, Joe. I'm for bed." Smiler began to move.

Joe said, "Sure there's nothin' wrong? Nothin' that you'd care to tell me about?"

"No, really, Joe. I'm all right."

"All right then, me old cock," said Joe. "Up you go then, and get your head tucked under your wing."

So Smiler went to bed, and not long afterwards Joe did the same. The cubs up on the plain were already asleep. Miss Milly and Mrs. Lakey were driving home from the Collingwoods' dinner party. The Major and his wife were together in their sitting-room. The Major was having a small glass of brandy and looked very thoughtful.

After a moment, he said, "I don't suppose they would do it – but perhaps it would have been better if I'd made them promise not to."

"Promise what, dear?" asked his wife.

"Promise not to warn this Samuel Miles that the police will be coming for him early tomorrow morning."

"Really!" exclaimed Mrs. Collingwood. "I'm glad you didn't do any such thing! You would have lost two very good friends – and made me very angry. They wouldn't dream of such a thing!"

The Major said, "They're both very fond of him." He smiled suddenly. "And they're women – you never know with women. Not logical. Not when their emotions are roused."

"I think," said Mrs. Collingwood distantly,

"that you'd better leave that brandy and go to bed. You must be over-tired."

*　　*　　*

Yet, in a way that he would never have been able to guess, the Major was quite right about women. With some it is the heart and not the head that rules.

At four o'clock the next morning Smiler woke up. It was still some way off daybreak. He lay in bed, heavy-eyed.

As he did so there was a sudden sharp splatter of gravel against his window pane. Smiler sat up, puzzled. The noise of gravel came again and he realized that it must have been such a noise in the first place which had wakened him.

He got out of bed and crossed to the window and looked down. On the narrow path below he could make out a greyish form. Smiler opened the window.

"Johnny?" A pale face was turned up to him from below.

"Who's that?" he asked.

"Keep your voice down. It's me, Pat," came the answer in a whisper.

"What on earth are you doing here?"

"Come to warn you, Johnny. Get dressed and come on down and I'll tell you. Hurry, I got to cycle back home afore they wakes and finds I've been out."

"But I don't understand."

"Course you don't, stupid, until you come down and I can tell you," said Pat. "Hurry now."

Still puzzled, Smiler dressed in a hurry and went quietly downstairs so as not to wake Joe. Pat Bagnall, in jeans and a thick jumper, was waiting for him in front of the house. She came up to him quickly and took his arm.

"Now, you listen to me, Johnny, and don't interrupt 'cos I've got a lot to say, and I've got to say it fast so's I can get back and not get into trouble."

Then she told him about the Collingwoods' dinner party and how her mother always on such occasions went down to help. Her mother, while taking things into the dining-room, had overheard the conversation about Samuel Miles, alias Johnny Pickering, through the open windows. When her mother had got back that night she had told her husband all about it, full of the gossip and excitement. Pat – who wasn't supposed to hear – had heard everything, too, because she had been up in her bedroom reading before sleep.

"When it's all quiet-like you can hear every word they say down below. So that's why I'm here. I had to wait till late to come out – and I got to get back fast before Dad starts moving."

"Crikeys!" said Smiler. "What am I going to do?"

"Don't be stupid," whispered Pat. "You got to get away. You don't want to be taken up again, do you?"

"No, of course I don't."

"Then you've got to move fast. Right now. Get your things and go."

And Smiler saw that he had to do just that. The Major might wake very early and call the police.

"It's all right," he said. "I was planning to go – tomorrow. Thanks for coming to tell me. But why ever did you?"

"What a question! Because I like you, of course. And because I don't believe that grown-ups always can do what they say they can do. I reckoned it was up to you to choose. Course, you can stay and face it out if you want to."

"Not likely. I'm off. Only my Dad can clear me up. He knows how to deal with Mr. Pickering and that lot. Gosh, it was brave of you to come."

"Course it wasn't. You got money, and things like that?"

"Yes."

"Then be on your way, Johnny. And Johnny –"

She came closer to him.

"Yes?"

"When you're settled – you can write to me, if you want."

Her face came close to Smiler's.

"Course I will when it's safe."

"Promise?"

"Promise."

She reached forward suddenly and kissed him. Then, with a little bubble of laughter, she was gone, running across the garden grass.

Smiler watched her go, not knowing quite how he felt, but knowing that he was feeling like he had never felt before. Then he turned and went quietly back into the house. All his things were more or less packed already for his Sunday morning departure. Now, he had to go a day sooner and there was a big problem. He *had* to get the key of Joe's van. Without the van his plan was ruined. Joe had not been to the Angel that night. Joe might wake up. Well, he would have to risk that.

He went up to his bedroom and collected his

things. He came out on tip-toes and put his stuff quietly on the floor of the little landing. In the darkness he moved stealthily towards the door of Joe's bedroom. He knew exactly where Joe's jacket would be hanging with the key in the pocket. The thought that Joe might wake brought a quick flush of sweat to his brow. Slowly he reached out his hand to the door knob.

At that moment the door of the bedroom opened and in the growing light from the bedroom window he was faced by the figure of Joe. Smiler jumped backwards, almost frightened out of his skin.

Joe said not a word. He just stood there. He wore an old woollen nightcap, and a long white nightshirt – but not so long that it hid the fact that he wore his socks in bed. Joe's eyes were shut tight.

Before Smiler could recover from his alarm, Joe began to speak in a far away kind of voice, a kind of religious, preaching voice.

Joe said, "Done it ever since a child. Doing of it now. Walks in me sleep. No cure for it. When I wakes up I don't know what I done – could be murder. Don't know what I heard – could be where a pot of gold's buried. Don't never know what I'm doing or hearing. Like I might 'ear two people talkin' under me window. Like I might know one of them's in trouble and got to get away fast and far. And for which purpose – as all the world knows – there's nought better'n a car. Say a nice little green van what the police'll find somewheres later and return. That's always assumin' that the one what wants it 'as the key –"

His hand came out and up slowly and the palm opened. In it was the van's ignition key.

"Oh, Joe —" began Smiler, but Joe interrupted him sharply.

"Don't never talk to anyone what walks in 'is sleep. Dangerous. Could give 'em the jumps for the rest of their mortal. Here, lad."

The key was tossed to Smiler who caught it.

Joe stood there, immobile, but a smile slowly passed over his face. One eye opened and shut in a wink, and he said, "Don't ever remember anything I says or does when I walks in me sleep. Terrible affliction if you lives on a cliff. Well, God bless anyone within 'earing at this moment — and send me a postcard sometime just saying — 'The old grey goose ain't dead'."

He winked once more, with the other eye, and then turned back into the room and shut the door. With tears in his eyes and a lump in his throat, Smiler picked up his stuff and ran downstairs and out into the yard. Five minutes later he was driving towards Heytesbury on his way up to the plain. It was Saturday and too early in the morning for the Vedette hut to be manned or for any troops to be about. Smiler knew that he had a clear two or three hours before anyone would be astir to bother him. That was more than enough.

* * *

Tonks saw the green van go by Danebury House and barked his head off until Mrs. Lakey, half in sleep, reached for a cushion and nearly knocked him from the window seat.

Pat Bagnall was back in bed, lying awake and dreaming. Down below she could hear her father stirring in the kitchen.

At Ford Cottage the barn owl had just returned from its night duties, full of food. In the cottage Major Collingwood was lying flat on his back, mouth open and snoring loudly. Mrs. Collingwood pushed him over on to his side and said loudly, "Quiet!" The Major became silent.

In her bedroom at Danebury Miss Milly lay awake having a little cry to herself and wrestling with temptation. She wanted to get up and drive to Joe's cottage to warn Johnny. But she knew she could not do it. She was a woman of honour, and anyway in the long run it would all be for Johnny's good. After a while she started to chuckle to herself. Fancy never guessing that Johnny dyed his hair! Right under her nose, too. Perhaps she needed glasses.

And in Joe's cottage, Joe lay abed and chuckled, too. They wouldn't see Johnny for smoke. No more than they had ever seen *him* for smoke when he had run away from the Army. Some things you just had to run away from. Just as there was some things you just had to run towards. . . . Like a bit of poaching or a nice pint of cider. Good lad, Johnny was. Wonder whatever it was that made him so fond of the plain? Not a girl, that was sure, 'cos there was none up there. Animals, he'd bet. . . . Just loved animals, Johnny did. God bless him.

14

↶ Hail and Farewell ↷

At the Vedette hut Smiler got out of the van and lifted the road pole. He drove through and then went back and lowered the pole.

From the hut the road ran due north to drop finally into the Imber valley. By now Smiler knew all the roads and tracks like the back of his hand.

The sky was lightening fast. The pearl-gold flush in the eastern sky was beginning to strengthen with the coming of the sun. The larks were already aloft and in first song. A pair of greenfinches flirted across the road in front of the van. A kestrel hovered over the tank which Yarra had first used as a shelter, watching for the movement of mice around its rusted sides. There was a heavy dew over the grass and the spiders' webs, hung from thistle to thistle and mantling the small bushes, were beaded with glittering moisture drops. High in the morning sky a jet fighter drew a long, straight vapour trail which began to rag away at the edges into little curls of cloud.

Within ten minutes Smiler was at Imber. He drove the van under the cover of the open barn at the rear of Imber Court. Taking his old haversack in which he had brought some dogs' meat, he walked around the side of Imber Court towards the valley in which the cubs lived. Under the tall trees at the foot of the valley a grey squirrel scurried away from him and raced up one of the trunks. The pack of jackdaws from the church tower flew overhead. The lip of the rising sun broke the edge of the far plain, throwing long bush and tree shadows.

Smiler walked up the valley bottom, alongside the tank tracks. He tried not to think that it was the last time he would go up to the den. Instead, he thought of how good Pat and Joe had been to him last night. Going by Danebury and hearing Tonks bark had been a bad moment. He was leaving all the animals there. Then, as he began to climb the steep slope to the cave plateau, he could think of nothing else but Yarra. He sniffed hard. Yarra had gone for good. And now he was going . . . right away, miles away. Because he felt so miserable, he gave himself a good talking-to. It's no good, Samuel M., he said, snivelling about things. Life is always changing. Like Joe said, if it didn't, then men would grow moss on 'em – just like the rocks.

At the den mouth he pulled up the planks and Afra and Rico came leaping out to him. They had heard his whistle as he came up the slope. The sight of them cheered him up at once.

They were well grown now and their tawny, spotted coats rippled and caught the day's new light as they moved. Afra had a creamy mantle showing under her neck. Rico's tail was long and drooping and could give you quite a crack if he happened to swing it across your face when you knelt to fondle him.

He dropped to his knees and played with them for a moment or two. After a while Rico, always the greedier, began to worry and paw at the haversack on Smiler's back.

"All right, my beauties," said Smiler. "A walk first and then food."

He started off down the steep slope, back towards Imber. Rico raced ahead and began mouse-hunting from tuft to tuft of grass. Afra found a tattered little white parachute from an old signal flare, picked it up and carried it for a while.

The birds and the beasts of the little valley watched them go. The three buzzards, low flying at the ridge-top, soared and hung over them. The carrion crow, dealing with a dead rabbit on the far slope, looked up and watched their movements and wondered what Afra was carrying. A deer couched in bracken followed them with large, liquid eyes. A hare got up well ahead of Rico and raced away followed by the cub. But there was no fear in the hare because it had more speed than Rico. The cub soon gave up the chase and came galloping back at the sound of Smiler's whistle. A pair of yellow hammers scolded them from an ash tree and a grass snake fifty yards ahead slid away to safety as it caught the thud, thud of Smiler's approaching footsteps.

At the small spring, which was now down to a feeble trickle, Smiler let the cubs drink. When they had taken their fill, they followed him up to the van.

He opened one of the back doors of the van, took meat from his haversack and tossed it inside. Rico jumped in immediately for the food, but Afra stood her ground for a moment or two. She sniffed around the back of the van and Smiler wondered whether he was going to have trouble with her. He took another piece of meat, held it briefly under Afra's nose, and then jerked it into the van as she made a move for it. Afra leaped into the van after the meat.

Smiler closed the door and locked it. He went round and got into the driving seat. The back part of the van was boarded off from the front. At some time Joe had made a small hatchway in it so that he could reach back and take things from the interior without getting out. The hatchway was fastened with small bolts, top and bottom. Smiler made sure that they were secure and then drove off.

He went back through the shattered, derelict village. Beyond the village, instead of taking the right-hand turn which led to the Heytesbury Vedette hut, he carried straight on.

The road rose up a gentle slope and came out on to the wide, open stretches of grass land. Half a mile down the road he turned left at a crossroads and began to bump his way along a narrow, rutted track. After a while the surface of the track grew better. Some minutes later Smiler was driving down the northern scarp of the plain, not far from the spot where Yarra had been attacked by the Ayrshire cow. He passed another empty Vedette hut. A little later he was off the plain near a small village called Erlestoke through which ran a main road. Smiler turned the van left-handed, westwards along the road. A mile along the main road, he drew up. He slipped the hatch bolts and peeped through at the cubs. There was straw in the van for them to lie on. They both came to the hatchway. Smiler rubbed their masks and then pushed through some more meat from his haversack.

He bolted the hatchway and drove on. He knew exactly where he was going, and he knew all the roads from the many drives he had taken with Joe. As soon as he could he left the main road. By now the police might be at Joe's cottage. If Joe couldn't keep from them the fact that the van was missing the police would put out a call for it. Well, if they did, they did. That was a risk he had to take.

In fact, he need not have worried. When the police came to Joe's cottage, Joe had been long up. He had taken Smiler's bicycle, wheeled it to the river and thrown it in. When the police arrived Joe at once told them that Johnny and his bicycle were gone. Which he could truthfully do. The police never asked him about his van. Joe reported its loss at mid-day when he went to the Angel.

*   *   *

Later that morning, not long after Longleat Park had been opened to the public, Apollo, the cheetah male, who had been the mate of Yarra, lay along the bare length of a branch of the fallen tree not far from the sleeping hut.

The sky was cloudless. Now and then Apollo raised his head and blinked in the strong light. Across the road and the grass two or three other cheetahs were pacing up and down the wire enclosure, their eyes on the free parkland beyond, the parkland over which Yarra long ago had escaped.

A few early cars were beginning to trickle through the animal enclosures now. Apollo watched them come around the curve of road which held the fallen tree. They had no interest for him. Every day he saw them. They usually stopped a little higher up the road from the tree where they could get a good view of the whole enclosure.

Apollo yawned and wrinkled his mask, then

snapped at a worrying blue bottle fly. One of the cheetahs by the fence flopped to the grass and began to roll on it, its long legs high in the air. A nuthatch landed on the far end of the old tree and began to work its way around and along a branch with short, jerky movements. Apollo watched it, half made to rise and then subsided. It was hot. He swung his long tail and thumped the tree trunk. The nuthatch flew off.

At that moment a small green van came around the curve of the road behind Apollo, turned up the little slope and then drew in to the side of the road. It was about twenty yards upwind of Apollo. Apollo watched it.

In the van was Smiler. He knew all about Longleat Park and its animal kingdom. This was the place that Joe had brought him to for his treat. On that day, when they had got as far as the cheetah enclosure, it was as much as Smiler could do not to tell Joe all about Yarra and her cubs. He had made Joe stay a long time in the enclosure, the other cars drawing out and passing them.

Now Smiler had returned bringing with him, safely hidden in the van, as he had long planned, Afra and Rico. They were now out of the cub stage, were young cheetahs.

Smiler looked across at Apollo, and the size and beauty of the animal made him think of Yarra. Behind him Afra and Rico moved restlessly in the van. The various animal scents that had come to them as they had passed through the other enclosures had roused them.

Smiler sat for a moment wishing he didn't have to go on with his plan, but knowing he must. It was the best thing for the cheetahs. Once it was done, he knew that he could not hang about and see how Afra and Rico would be received. He would have to move on because at the entry to the enclosure he had seen one of the black and white Land-Rovers of the Game Wardens.

Smiler turned and drew the bolts on the hatch. You've got to do it, Samuel M., he told himself. You've just got to do it.

He opened the hatch wide. Afra and Rico came to the opening. Smiler held up a piece of meat he had saved and then leaned over and quietly opened the door of the cab.

Rico slid through the hatchway and went for the meat Smiler held. Before Rico could take it, Smiler threw it out on to the grass. Rico jumped out after it.

Afra came through the hatchway after her brother and sat on the seat at his side. She looked out at Rico.

"Go on, Afra, go on!" urged Smiler. But Afra sat on her haunches, twisted her neck, and rubbed the top of her head against Smiler's shoulder.

"Afra, please," Smiler pleaded. Afra sat where she was. Desperate, Smiler eased himself sideways and pushed Afra off the seat to the floor. She turned briefly, spat-snapped nervously at him and then lifted her muzzle. A mixture of new and familiar scents came flooding through the open door. She jumped down on to the grass to join Rico.

Relieved, Smiler pulled the door shut and drove off. He drove, sniffing and fighting back the tears which pressed against the back of his eyes. He went up the road as fast as he could without drawing attention to himself. As he went he watched Afra and Rico in the mudguard mirror. Rico was couched on the grass, chewing at his piece of meat. Afra was standing up, slowly swinging her blunt head and long neck as she looked around the enclosure.

A turn in the road at the top of the enclosure took them both from Smiler's sight, and he told himself, You've looked after the cubs, Samuel M. You've done the right thing. Now you start thinking about yourself.

* * *

Apollo was the first living thing in the enclosure to see the young cheetahs. Even before he saw them he had caught their scent coming downwind to him. As the van drew away they came into view. His head jerked up alertly. Slowly he raised himself to a stalking position and began to move out along the length of the fallen tree trunk. At the end he stopped, watching Afra standing and looking round, seeing Rico on the ground worrying at the meat. Their scent was strange, but it was cheetah scent. Cheetahs in captivity do not always take kindly to the introduction of new members.

Suddenly Apollo leapt from the end of the trunk in a long, curving spring. Ignoring the few cars that moved up the road, he walked slowly, deliberately across to the young cheetahs. Afra turned and faced him and then dropped her shoulders and opened her jaws in a silent gape, half-menace, half-fear. Rico looked up from his meat and rumbled a caution for Apollo to keep away.

By the fence the other cheetahs had caught the new scent. Slowly they began to move towards the young cheetahs, not directly, but in small, exploratory arcs.

Apollo moved to Rico and lowered his head. Rico – Apollo's own son – snapped at the big male to guard his meat. Apollo's right forepaw swept out and cuffed Rico away from the meat. Rico rolled over and over for about a yard. He came to his feet, shook himself and then moved confidently back to his meat. Apollo had done to him no more than Yarra had sometimes done.

Apollo watched Rico come back and drop to the meat, almost under his muzzle. For a moment Apollo's paw rose and then the movement stopped. He let Rico take the meat, and turned. Afra was standing just behind him. Ten yards away the other cheetahs had bunched together, some standing, some squatting, all watching Apollo. All of them knew the power of Apollo and respected him.

Slowly Apollo lowered his head and sniffed at Afra, who now stood timidly still. She made a small complaining sound. Apollo squatted back on his haunches. He yawned, raising his head and blinking at the sun, and then he dropped flat to the ground, head and shoulders high, facing the other cheetahs. Afra squatted a foot from him. Rico ate behind him. The cars passed slowly along the road, and the other cheetahs, as though they had been given some command dangerous to disobey, slowly turned and moved away.

Apollo had accepted Afra and Rico. Father, son and daughter were together.

*   *   *

POSTSCRIPT: *Joe's old green van was found by the police late that afternoon. It was abandoned in a lay-by on a main road twenty miles from Longleat. Lying on the driving seat was a note that read:*

This van belongs to Joe Ringer of Heytesbury. Say to him the old grey goose is still flying.

General Editors: Anne and Ian Serraillier

Chinua Achebe Things Fall Apart
Vivien Alcock The Cuckoo Sister; The Monster Garden; The Trial of Anna Cotman
Michael Anthony Green Days by the River
Bernard Ashley High Pavement Blues; Running Scared
J G Ballard Empire of the Sun
Stan Barstow Joby
Nina Bawden On the Run; The Witch's Daughter; A Handful of Thieves; Carrie's War; The Robbers; Devil by the Sea; Kept in the Dark; The Finding; Keeping Henry
Judy Blume It's Not the End of the World; Tiger Eyes
E R Braithwaite To Sir, With Love
F Hodgson Burnett The Secret Garden
Ray Bradbury The Golden Apples of the Sun
Betsy Byars The Midnight Fox
Victor Canning The Runaways; Flight of the Grey Goose
John Christopher The Guardians; Empty World
Gary Crew The Inner Circle
Jane Leslie Conly Racso and the Rats of NIMH
Roald Dahl Danny, The Champion of the World; The Wonderful Story of Henry Sugar; George's Marvellous Medicine; The BFG; The Witches; Boy; Going Solo; Charlie and the Chocolate Factory
Andrew Davies Conrad's War
Anita Desai The Village by the Sea
Peter Dickinson The Gift; Annerton Pit; Healer
Berlie Doherty Granny was a Buffer Girl
Gerald Durrell My Family and Other Animals
J M Falkner Moonfleet
Anne Fine The Granny Project
F Scott Fitzgerald The Great Gatsby
Anne Frank The Diary of Anne Frank
Leon Garfield Six Apprentices
Graham Greene The Third Man and The Fallen Idol; The Power and the Glory; Brighton Rock

Marilyn Halvorson Cowboys Don't Cry
Thomas Hardy The Withered Arm and Other Wessex Tales
Rosemary Harris Zed
L P Hartley The Go-Between
Esther Hautzig The Endless Steppe
Ernest Hemingway The Old Man and the Sea; A Farewell to Arms
Nat Hentoff Does this School have Capital Punishment?
Nigel Hinton Getting Free; Buddy; Buddy's Song
Minfong Ho Rice Without Rain
Janni Howker Badger on the Barge; Isaac Campion
Monica Hughes Ring-Rise, Ring-Set
Shirley Hughes Here Comes Charlie Moon
Kristin Hunter Soul Brothers and Sister Lou
Barbara Ireson (Editor) In a Class of Their Own
Jennifer Johnston Shadows on Our Skin
Toeckey Jones Go Well, Stay Well
James Joyce A Portrait of the Artist as a Young Man
Geraldine Kaye Comfort Herself; A Breath of Fresh Air
Clive King Me and My Million
Dick King-Smith The Sheep-Pig
Daniel Keyes Flowers for Algernon
Elizabeth Laird Red Sky In the Morning
D H Lawrence The Fox and The Virgin and the Gypsy; Selected Tales
Harper Lee To Kill a Mockingbird
Laurie Lee As I Walked Out One Midsummer Morning
Julius Lester Basketball Game
Ursula Le Guin A Wizard of Earthsea
C Day Lewis The Otterbury Incident
David Line Run for Your Life; Screaming High
Joan Lingard Across the Barricades; Into Exile; The Clearance; The File on Fraulein Berg
Penelope Lively The Ghost of Thomas Kempe
Jack London The Call of the Wild; White Fang
Lois Lowry The Road Ahead; The Woods at the End of Autumn Street
Bernard Mac Laverty Cal; The Best of Bernard Mac Laverty
Margaret Mahy The Haunting; The Catalogue of The Universe
Jan Mark Thunder and Lightning; Under the Autumn Garden

How many have you read?